THE VI
AND
THE SAMURAI

The inside story of the collaboration between
British Leyland/Rover and Honda

John Bacchus

The Viking and the Samurai, first published 2024
by the Rover 200 and 400 Owners Club; rover200.org.uk

Printed by Short Run Press

Editing, picture research and captions, design and layout by Gillian Bardsley

John Bacchus is hereby identified as the author of this work in accordance with section 77 of the Copyrights, Designs and Patents Act 1988.

All rights reserved

No part of this publication may be reprinted or reproduced, or utilised in any form by any electronic, mechanical or other means, now known or hereafter invented, including photocopying, digitisation and recording, or held in any storage or retrieval system, without the prior permission in writing of John Bacchus or any other copyright holders named herein.

© John Bacchus 2024

Profits from this publication will be donated to Dementia Research UK
207 Regent Street, London, W1B 3HH; demruk.org.uk

ISBN 978-1-3999-8614-4

CONTENTS

		Page
Introductory Note and Acknowledgments		4
List of Illustrations		5
Foreword	By Gillian Bardsley	7
Introduction	A Note from the Author	9
Chapter 1	Background	11
Chapter 2	Early Contacts	13
Chapter 3	1978/79: Getting Underway	17
Chapter 4	1979: Bounty Is Launched	27
Chapter 5	1979/80: A Change of Direction	31
Chapter 6	1981: An Eventful Year	43
Chapter 7	1982: A Busy Year	47
Chapter 8	1983: A Year of Agreements	53
Chapter 9	1984: Gathering Momentum	63
Chapter 10	1985: Focus on Engines	67
Chapter 11	1986: Things Get Hectic!	77
Chapter 12	1987: The Year of Quality!	85
Chapter 13	1988: Privatisation	93
Chapter 14	1989: Making it Legal at Last	103
Chapter 15	1990: Easter in New York	109
Chapter 16	1991: The 'S-K' Projects	113
Chapter 17	1992: Synchro Goes Live	117
Chapter 18	1993: British Aerospace Heads for the Exit	121
Chapter 19	1994: The Twilight of the Gods	131
Conclusion	Reflections from the Vantage Point of 1996	133
Appendix 1	Focus on the Cars (by Ian Elliott)	137
Appendix 2	John Bacchus Timeline	154
Appendix 3	A Short History of Collaboration (by John Bacchus)	155
Bibliography		157
Index		159

INTRODUCTORY NOTE

This text is presented as John Bacchus wrote and completed it in 1996. It therefore reflects his views at that moment in time. There is no postscript about 'what happened afterwards' because this is not part of his story. For those who would like to learn about subsequent events, the Bibliography contains details of books which will inform the reader about the BMW era and beyond. An overview of John's career can be found in Appendix 2.

ACKNOWLEDGMENTS

This book has been brought to publication by a team of people who are eager to see this unique story added to the resources available to automotive historians and car enthusiasts. The manuscript was originally brought to John Batchelor's attention through the Austin Rover/Rover Group Alumni. John sought the permission of Richard Bacchus to proceed, and chance meetings with the other members of the team brought on board the necessary range of skills.

- *Richard Bacchus* is the son of John Bacchus. He has managed the Heritage Certificate Service for the British Motor Industry Heritage Trust since 2002.
- *John Batchelor* is a retired automotive engineer, Chairman of the Rover 200 and 400 Owners Club, and Administrator of the Austin Rover/Rover Group Alumni.
- *Gillian Bardsley* is a published author and historian of the automotive industry. She was Archivist to the British Motor Industry Heritage Trust for 30 years. On retirement she became Honorary Historian to the Trust.
- *Ian Elliott* worked in the Public Relations Department of British Leyland/Rover from 1973 to 1991 (much of the period covered by this narrative) before becoming a freelance technical/marketing writer.
- *Denis Chick* has a lifetime's experience in the motor industry and particularly PR, including British Leyland/Rover Group.

Thanks go to Colin Corke for help with research and proof-reading, Richard Dredge for assistance with picture research and original photography, Sarah Jane Wilson of the BMIHT Archive Department for expertly scanning additional material for the illustrations and Stephen Laing, Head of Collections at the British Motor Museum.

ILLUSTRATIONS by kind permission of:

British Motor Industry Heritage Trust (britishmotormuseum.co.uk):
    all except as indicated below
Magic Car Pics (magiccarpics.co.uk):
    front cover, 26 (middle right), 36, 76 (middle), 99 (bottom), 100-101,
    127 (top), 129 (middle and bottom), 136 (right hand column)
Richard Dredge: 38 (middle), 130 (top)
Denis Chick: 153
Richard Bacchus: back cover, 130 (bottom), 152
Gillian Bardsley: 8 (Chart)

LIST OF ILLUSTRATIONS

	Page
Development and breakup of British Leyland/Rover Group, 1968-95	8
John Bacchus in 1976	9
The British Leyland product range, 1976	12
Harold Wilson, Labour Prime Minister	26
Margaret Thatcher, Conservative Prime Minister	26
Michael Edwardes, Chairman of British Leyland, 1977-82	26
Kiyoshi Kawashima, President of Honda, 1973-83	26
David Andrews, Finance Director, British Leyland	26
Mark Snowdon, Managing Director, Austin Rover	26
Harold Musgrove, Chairman, Austin Rover	26
Honda Civic and CVCC engine, 1972/73	36
Honda Civic in London, 1974	36
Rover SD1 on a test rig, 1977	37
LM11 (Austin Montego) in the Longbridge Design Studio, circa 1980	37
Signing the first joint agreement, December 1979	38
Early Triumph Acclaim on view at Longbridge, 1981	38
Triumph Acclaim production at Cowley, 1981	39-41
Triumph Acclaim, cutaway illustration	41
Signing the XX Agreement, November 1981	42
Press conference following the signing, November 1981	42
Styling model, British Leyland version of XX (Rover 800), June 1982	58
Design sketches, Honda version of XX (Legend), July 1982	58
Styling model, Honda version of XX (Legend), September 1982	59
Design sketch, 'Acclaim Facelift' (Rover 200/Honda Ballade)	59
Clay model, Honda version of 'Acclaim Facelift' (Ballade), June 1983	60
British Leyland version of 'Acclaim Facelift' (Rover 200), 1983	60
Rover 200 production at Longbridge, 1984	61-62
Rover 216 Vitesse, 1986	61
Roland Bertodo and his team with the M16 engine, 1987	66
K-series engine: 1.4-litre (1984) and KV6 (1996)	66
Rover 800 production at Cowley, 1986	72-73
Austin Rover booklet, *Tomorrow Today*	74
Rover 800, cutaway illustration	74
Margaret Thatcher helps to promote the Rover 800, 1986	75

LIST OF ILLUSTRATIONS (continued)   *Page*

Graham Day, Chairman of Rover Group, 1986-91	76
George Simpson, Chairman of Rover Group, 1991-94	76
Tadashi Kume, President of Honda, 1983-90	76
Nobuhiko Kawamoto, President of Honda, 1990-98	76
Les Wharton, Managing Director, Rover Group	76
Tony Rose, Finance Director, Rover Group	76
John Towers, Managing Director, Rover Group	76
A Rover delegation visits Honda's Suzuka factory, 1989	96
Signing of Statement of Understanding, July 1989	96
Honda Concerto saloon on view at Canley, 1988	97
Dinoc clay model, Synchro styling concept (Rover 600), 1989	97
Rover 200 (R8) production at Longbridge, 1989	98
Rover 400 and 200 (R8) comparison, 1990	98
Honda Concerto production at Longbridge	99
HUM Swindon publicity leaflet, 1992	99
HUM Swindon vehicle assembly, 1993-95	100-101
Longbridge-built Concerto being tested by Honda	101
Rover 800 facelift (R17), cutaway illustration	102
Styling sketches for the Rover grille design, 1991	102
Rover 600 (Synchro), 1993	126
Honda Accord with a GWR steam locomotive, 1992	127
End of Honda Concerto production at Longbridge	127
Styling models, Rover 400 (HHR), September 1989	128
Rover 400 (HHR) publicity shot, 1995	128
Land Rover Discovery (1989) and Honda Crossroad (1993)	129
Mr Kawamoto with a Honda Civic at the Paris Motor Show, 1994	129
Gifts given to John Bacchus on his retirement, January 1995	130
John Bacchus as a guest at Shuko Hayashi's retirement, 1998	130
The complete range of British Leyland/Rover/Honda models	136
Austin Allegro launch in Spain, 1973	152
British Motor Show at Earls Court, 1975	152
Launch of the Sterling in the USA, 1988	153

FOREWORD

As recorded in this memoir, John Bacchus retired from Rover Group in January 1995. John had negotiated and nurtured the Anglo-Japanese partnership for 16 years. He survived all the turmoil of the British Leyland/Rover Group years, the 'night of the long knives' sackings, and saw it through from the beginning to the end. In 1994, British Aerospace decided to sell Rover Group to BMW, a move which caused Honda to step back from the relationship, though the products the two companies had developed together continued to be produced under licence. This was an obvious moment for those connected to the Honda relationship to step back and look for new projects of their own to pursue.

At that time I was Archivist to the British Motor Industry Heritage Trust, which is the custodian of extensive Archive and Vehicle Collections, much of which originated from British Leyland. Only two years previously, Rover Group had built the Heritage Motor Centre next to their proving ground in Gaydon to house these collections. It has since changed its name to the British Motor Museum.

It was my good fortune that the project John settled on that year was to write a biographical memoir. Our Managing Director was Fred Coultas, an ex-Rover engineer and an old friend of John's, who invited him to Gaydon and introduced us. It was agreed that he would work with me, with the full resources of the Archive at his disposal. He settled down on a desk next to mine and began to type his story on an old-fashioned word processor. He gave it the title *The Viking and the Samurai* and produced a fascinating account of historic events from a unique perspective. It was not about product ranges or management battles. Instead it was a human account of what is was like to be an integral part of building this innovative relationship with a key player in the emerging Japanese car industry.

After finishing the memoir, John continued to contribute to the Archive's work. He used his expert knowledge of the industry to assist in cataloguing a broad range of important material. In the early 2000s he decided to concentrate on his work with the Warwick Manufacturing Group, but he kept his links with the Trust as a Trustee, a role he retained until 2007. I myself retired in 2019.

During the years we worked together, he became a mentor to me at a point in my career when I was relatively new to my role and learning to navigate managing an Archive and all that entailed. His experience, even-headedness, negotiating skills, good nature, sense of humour and sage advice all stood me in good stead long after he had moved on to other projects. I am forever grateful to him.

Gillian Bardsley
Worcester, 2024

DEVELOPMENT AND BREAK-UP OF BRITISH LEYLAND/ROVER GROUP 1968-1995

Chief Executive Officer (CEO)	HOLDING COMPANY
1968 Donald Stokes	**BRITISH LEYLAND MOTOR CORPORATION LTD 1968** Original Holding Company
1975 Alex Park	**BRITISH LEYLAND LTD 1975** New Holding Company set up following the Ryder Report, British Government 99.8% shareholder

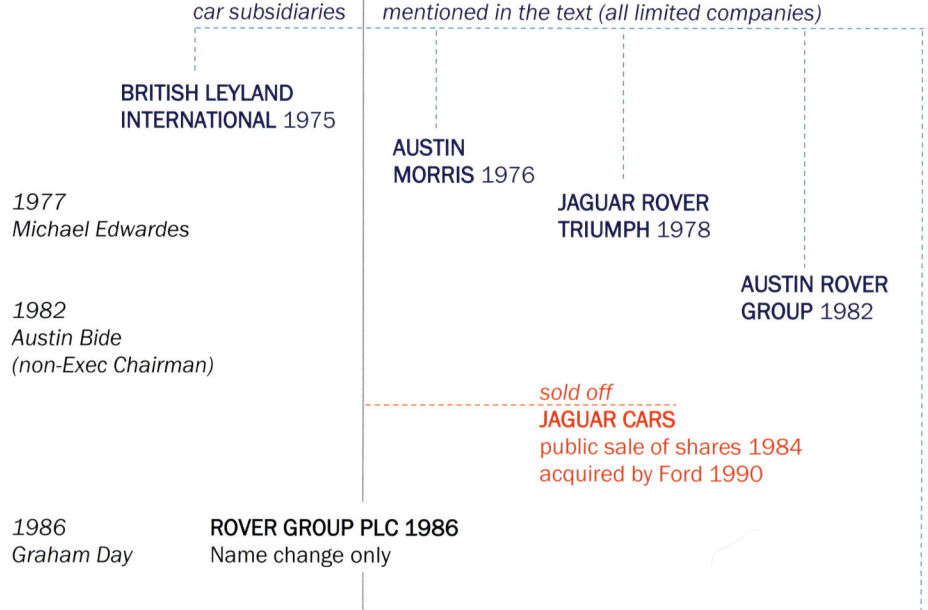

1977 Michael Edwardes	
1982 Austin Bide (non-Exec Chairman)	
1986 Graham Day	**ROVER GROUP PLC 1986** Name change only
	ROVER GROUP HOLDINGS LTD 1988 Sold to British Aerospace
1991 George Simpson	
	BMW UK HOLDINGS LTD 1995 Sold to BMW AG

NOTE:
In terms of subsidiaries, there was not a steady progression from one to another. A new company would be set up, but the old one would remain and be allowed to go dormant. The general pattern was of a Central Board (the Holding Company) with different parts of the business being delegated to Subordinate Boards (the Subsidiaries).

INTRODUCTION
A note from the author

John Bacchus in 1976

The story which follows is about a very unusual and historically significant collaboration between two independent and competing motor companies, Rover and Honda. Because I was intimately involved from its conception, it will, I hope, provide an interesting human perspective of this very longstanding relationship. It cannot be a fully comprehensive picture, the relationship became very complex and it was impossible to keep involved in all the operational details. Many other people could give their experiences of aspects of it which are not covered here. My objective is to give a personal view of the development of the relationship, as seen from a privileged position which extended over a period of 16 years. It is not an impartial view; my belief in the overall value of the relationship to British Leyland/Rover was constant and remains. There were some who did not share that view, with them I can only register my disagreement.

There are occasional references in the story to things which I was doing, either before getting involved with Honda or whilst involved with them. This is because, although the management of the relationship has been a constant, for much of the time covered by the story it was a very important part of a wider responsibility.

My entire working life has been spent in the motor industry. It is in my genes. My father was in the motor trade all his life and, as a result, I was brought up with, and always loved cars of all types. The only period away was when I left school and went to do a commercial apprenticeship at Rolls-Royce Aero Division. As soon as I qualified, however, I left to join Ford, where I remained from 1960 to 1966, working first in the central finance staff and later in the product planning organisation. In 1966 I was tempted away from Ford to join Rootes, shortly after its takeover by Chrysler. Two years were spent there in financial management positions and then, completely disaffected by the contrast between Chrysler and Ford, I welcomed the opportunity to move to the recently formed British Leyland Motor Corporation (BLMC) in 1969. The company underwent many changes of identity during my time there. For simplicity I will refer to it either as British Leyland or, after 1986, Rover Group. In the 25-plus years which I spent there my roles were always concerned with financial, product, and strategic/business planning matters on the car side of the business.

It must be emphasised that, throughout the period covered in this story, I have been supported by a splendid group of people. It is not possible to mention everyone but, in the context of the Honda relationship, my closest colleagues for the last ten years of my working life at Rover were 'The Honda Team'; namely Ray Anderson, Moira Barbour, Peter McVeigh and David Puckering. They, jointly and severally, supported and assisted me and kept me pointing in more or less the right direction. I have not kept referring to them in the text; however, nearly everything which was done involved them and I remain eternally grateful to them for their unflagging support, assistance and companionship. Their part in keeping the enormously complex relationship on the rails cannot be overstated and this story should stand as a tribute to them and to all the other people, in both companies, who succeeded in making work something which many people would have declared unworkable.

John Bacchus, 1996

Chapter 1
BACKGROUND
Why do we need a partner?

Before starting my story, I should explain the situation which, in 1978, caused the British Leyland Board to seek substantial collaborative links with another car manufacturer.

It all happened some time ago, and in very different circumstances to those which now exist. We were about to start the 'Thatcher Years', having lived through the economic turmoil of the 1970s, which saw a rapid escalation in inflation affecting people's living standards. This was compounded by nightmare industrial relations, and of all the areas which suffered that nightmare, the motor industry was probably the worst. British Leyland was the epicentre of the UK motor industry and became a byword for industrial strife.

The British Leyland Motor Corporation (BLMC) had been formed in 1968 by a merger of British Motor Holdings and the Leyland Motor Corporation instigated by the Labour Government. British Motor Holdings was a combination of previous mergers between Austin, Morris, MG, Jaguar and Pressed Steel while the Leyland Motor Corporation incorporated Rover, Triumph and Leyland Motors. In fact, this latest event was really a takeover of the very large British Motor Holdings by the much smaller, but superficially healthier, Leyland Motor Corporation.

It was full of problems and the company's fragile position became untenable in 1974, following the economic and industrial problems created by the miners' strike of that year. Faced with the potential insolvency of one of the country's major industrial groups, the newly re-elected Labour Government led by Harold Wilson initiated a review of the company's situation. Known as the Ryder Report after Sir Don Ryder, the industrialist called in to carry out the investigation, this report recommended major investment in BLMC to establish it as a driver of the UK industrial base (a very similar approach to that taken by the French Government with Renault for many years). The report was adopted and the Government bought virtually all the BLMC shares. In 1975, it was renamed British Leyland Ltd and remained a limited company in which the majority shareholder was the Government. It was not a nationalised industry.

The company was vast; it built every type of vehicle, from Minis to giant Scammell trucks, and included cars, vans, 4x4s, trucks, buses, armoured military vehicles, specialised engines, construction equipment and so on among its product portfolio. It was truly international with major manufacturing operations in Belgium, Italy, Spain, South Africa, Australia, India, Iran, Nigeria, Kenya, Rhodesia and New Zealand. With its sports cars and Jaguars it also had a major sales presence in North America. There were about 170,000 employees in 1975.

The entire British Leyland product range pictured in 1976: 'cars, vans, 4x4s, trucks, buses, armoured military vehicles, construction equipment ...'

Chapter 2
EARLY CONTACTS
Someone has always done it before!

Although the British Leyland/Honda relationship as we know it commenced in 1978, there had been earlier contacts between the two companies.

In 1978, the Honda Motor Company was a relative newcomer to the car industry, having started production of its first 'motorcycle technology' minicar in 1963. Its first 'automobile technology' car, the Honda Civic, was not introduced until 1972. This vehicle launched Honda into the technological front rank of Japanese car manufacturers who were, at that time, very conventional in their design approach. Front-engine, rear-wheel drive was the norm, the aim being very specifically an American car of the period in miniature. The Civic was transverse-engined, front-wheel drive, with an all-aluminium power unit. In design concept it was thus aligned with what were then the most advanced European vehicles. They took this one step further by announcing the Compound Vortex Controlled Combustion (CVCC) engine which, to the disgust of the US automobile establishment, demonstrated that the US 1975 exhaust emission requirements could be met without destroying the industry or driving the price of the product beyond the reach of the customer.

Meanwhile, British Leyland was undergoing the upheavals resulting from the implementation of the Ryder Report in 1975. Part of the restructuring of the company recommended by the Ryder team, was that the International Division be substantially strengthened and made responsible for all British Leyland's activities outside the UK. Thus British Leyland International Ltd was established, with David Andrews as Managing Director.

British Leyland had a longstanding link with the New Zealand Motor Corporation (NZMC), which was the car assembler and distributor in New Zealand where British Motor Holdings had been a major player. By 1975, it held a significant shareholding in NZMC, which was beginning to feel the effect of both British Leyland's decline and new competition from Japan. As a result, it was operating at well below capacity and was having profitability problems. The company was building the Mini, Allegro, Marina and Maxi from components sent from the UK; but neither it, nor British Leyland, was making any money from the exercise.

It is worth noting that, whatever else British Leyland management could be accused of, it was not guilty of giving insufficient 'on territory' attention to its New Zealand subsidiary. In 1976 or 1977, the writer (who never did get to visit New Zealand) clearly recalls that the NZMC management sent a message to Leyland House (the headquarters of British Leyland and British Leyland International in Marylebone Road, London) requesting fewer visits from UK based people, as these visits were distracting them from sorting out the business!

Into this difficult situation came an approach from Honda: would NZMC build the Civic for sale in New Zealand? Although British Leyland International had reservations about this 'thin end of the wedge', it did not itself have a solution to NZMC's problems. Bluntly it had more pressing problems within its wholly owned subsidiaries in Europe and other parts of the world. This first step eventually developed into Honda taking a shareholding in NZMC and British Leyland divesting itself of its shareholding. This early, indirect contact did not, however, create a more significant relationship between the companies.

Research (ie fortuitous accident) has in fact revealed an earlier contact between the companies which was unknown to me until recently. In 1975, shortly after the re-organisation following the Ryder Report, a production engineering team visited Japan to study Japanese methods on the spot. They visited Toyota, Nissan, Mitsubishi and Honda. Listed amongst the people they met at Honda were Mr Fujio Ishikawa and Mr Kiyoshi Ikemi, both of whom subsequently came to play significant roles in the relationship. Little of note came out of this first contact and the trip report concentrated much more on Toyota and Nissan, which was quite understandable given Honda's new-boy status.

The next contact between the two companies came in 1977. During this period, I was Director of Car Business Plans for British Leyland International. Included in my responsibilities was that of representing the interests of the 'major companies' for car matters in the UK. These were the wholly owned subsidiaries outside Europe such as USA, Canada, South Africa and Australia. It was becoming increasingly difficult for these companies to develop viable corporate plans due to a lack of suitable car product, both currently and in the forward plans of the Leyland Cars Division (which was the name for the mass-market car-making operation within British Leyland). This was particularly true for what were then the substantial manufacturing locations in Australia and South Africa. What was needed for these markets was a truly competitive modern, mid-size, family car. This was not a product priority for Leyland Cars and plans for what eventually became Montego were then rather vague. By this time, however, these markets in particular were beginning to feel the real impact of Japanese competition.

British Leyland International Ltd had been established as a self-contained profit centre within British Leyland. The approach was to handle British Leyland products as the first priority. If, however, nothing suitable was available, then the assets could be used for the products of other manufacturers. As a result we had, for example, arranged to distribute Saab cars in Canada. In the summer of 1977 Mike Kemp, who worked with me, did a study reviewing other manufacturers and their products to assess their suitability and possible availability to our operations. The clear leader came out as a car which was not yet in production but which was known to be on the way. This was the first 4-door Honda Accord. The 3-door version of the Accord had been launched in 1976 and had rapidly enjoyed considerable success, particularly in the USA, reinforcing the success of the Civic which was already well established.

We thought that the best place to start was South Africa, as Honda were not represented there at that time and therefore the proposition that we build and sell the Accord might interest them. The idea was discussed with Peter Murrough, then Managing Director of Leyland South Africa. He was enthusiastic about the proposal and so we, the British Leyland International team, presented it to our Managing Director, David Andrews. He recognised the strength of the logic and the potential for such a project. By this time, however, he was facing a difficult financial situation in South Africa with an acute shortage of funding for car models, particularly for a project of this type, the investment for which would be additional to the Corporate Plan.

South Africa was at this time a very overheated car market. The annual market size was about 200,000, but there were about 14 manufacturers assembling cars, with a local content requirement of 67% by mass. Achievement of this necessitated major investment programmes for locally sourced bodies and engines. The industry was substantially over-capacitated and was, in fact, subsidised by the multinational parents in the belief that it would, one day, expand exponentially as the black and coloured communities came more heavily into car ownership.

David Andrews agreed to contact being made with Honda, but on the understanding that a deal would be possible only if Honda would agree to fund the tooling required to put the car into production. This seemed unlikely but it was still worth a try and so we contacted Honda in Tokyo and a meeting was set up. The timing coincided with the Tokyo Motor Show, and the establishment of British Leyland International's new sales company in Japan, which was a joint venture with Mitsui.

This was my first trip to Japan. It was via Japan Air Lines (JAL) using the 'Polar Route' through Anchorage. Later on this became my way to work, but in 1977 it was all an exciting new experience. Fellow 'Anchorageites' will remember 'Fred' the stuffed Polar Bear with affectionate nostalgia! This was unfortunately the only time I was able to fly into Haneda Airport which is comfortably close to central Tokyo. All subsequent trips took place after they had managed to get Narita Airport open. Narita is a pleasant enough modern airport, the problem is its distance of over 60 kilometres from downtown Tokyo. The length of the last lap to your hotel, particularly when the traffic is bad, seems to be the longest part of the whole trip.

In the event, the first British Leyland-Honda meeting, though cordial, did not have a successful outcome. Peter Murrough and I met Mr Shinomiya, a Senior Managing Director of Honda. Contrary to all the received wisdom about dealing with the Japanese, he had no reservations about stating their position. It quickly became clear that Honda was interested in the proposition and had no other plans for getting into the South African market, as Japanese law did not permit direct investment in South Africa. He was equally forthright in his reaction to the proposal that Honda should fund the tooling for the project - "No!" We could not find a way around the problem in the further discussion and we had a very clear brief from David. On our return to the UK, I did try to persuade David to change his mind since Honda was so keen and this might lead to further projects. The funding could not be found, however, and so I had to advise Mr Shinomiya that, with regret, we could not proceed. It was a great disappointment at that time; however, it had caused us to look very closely at, and develop a healthy respect for Honda's newly-developed car operations. This lay fallow for several more months until everything started up at a corporate level in 1978.

The final episode in the South African story occurred in 1981 when Honda advised me that it had done a deal with United Car and Diesel Distributors (UCDD), the Mercedes-Benz assemblers in South Africa, for them to build the Ballade which we were to produce as the Triumph Acclaim.

Chapter 3
1978/79: GETTING UNDERWAY
In which the world begins to change

Things had not been going well for British Leyland since it became a government-owned institution. The change of ownership did not solve the problems inside the company and, in late 1977, Michael Edwardes, then Chief Executive of Chloride Group, was brought in as Executive Chairman. He commenced the changes and the restructuring which eventually led to the company which came into being under the Rover Group banner during the 1980s. There was a very speedy recognition of the great need which the car operations had for expert assistance to provide new products and help with improving efficiency and quality. It was this recognition which led to the establishment of the partnership whose story is told here. It is not the intention of this work to review the history of British Leyland, other than to explain the background to the extent necessary to put the relationship with Honda into the proper context. Sir Michael's own book *Back from the Brink* provides a detailed story of the years 1977-1982 which cover the critical period during which it was initially being established.

Very quickly after his arrival, Michael Edwardes instituted a series of reviews of the state of the company. He also appointed David Andrews as Executive Vice-Chairman and Finance Director. The previous structure consisted of two Divisions – Leyland Cars and Truck & Bus – covering product supply and UK sales, with British Leyland International responsible for all offshore activities. This was changed. The new structure for cars recreated the former product companies in the guise of Austin Morris Ltd and Jaguar Rover Triumph Ltd. They would be responsible for supplying the products, and British Leyland Europe & Overseas was to be responsible for selling them everywhere. One of the conclusions quickly arrived at by the new Edwardes team was that the car operations, particularly Austin Morris, were short of up-to-date product. Not only that, but the new product which was in the pipeline was a long way off. Serious collaboration was required to provide some product input sooner than internal resources could provide. Work was already going on inside the company on possible collaboration. The truck operation had been seriously considering the possibility of joining in the IVECO truck consortium for some time and Leyland Cars had been having discussions with Renault. The Renault discussions had been broadly based, covering product and component possibilities, and had several working parties involved.

David Andrews now instituted a review of the collaborative possibilities for cars. The first port of call was, of course, the existing situation with Renault. It quickly transpired that, although the joint working parties had been operating for some time, there was little concrete to show for it. The main proposal from Renault was fatally flawed, the suggestion being that British Leyland should build a Renault car, possibly the Renault 18, and sell it through the British Leyland sales network. The flaw was that the offer applied only to the UK market, no export sales could be considered. As one of British Leyland's key objectives was to substantially expand its market in continental Europe, the Renault proposal did not provide a satisfactory solution.

The studies got seriously underway in early summer 1978 with the objective of establishing whether there were more attractive potential collaborative partners for the car operations. There was a reluctance at this stage to go for a Japanese partner because of concern about possible adverse external reactions. The first sweep was therefore aimed at identifying possible occidental partners.

This review concluded that Chrysler Europe presented a serious possibility. Chrysler's European operations had been established in the mid-1960s by the acquisition of the Rootes Group and Simca. Chrysler was thus very much the last of the US 'Big Three' to get seriously established in Europe and it had not been a happy experience for them. Although they were having difficulties, there were aspects of a potential collaboration which made them the preferred target. This recommendation was qualified, however, by a statement that if Japanese companies were to be included, then Honda would be the overall preference. The Board accepted the Chrysler recommendation and preparations were put in hand to set up a meeting between Michael Edwardes and the Chrysler corporate management. This process had, however, only just got underway when the announcement was made that Chrysler had sold its European operations to Peugeot. The so-called 'Dovetail' project was stillborn.

It was very swiftly agreed that, with the Chrysler route being closed, Honda should be approached and the risk of adverse external comment accepted. The matter was now regarded as urgent. Having been pipped at the post with Chrysler, there was a concern that Honda was the only one of the second-tier Japanese manufacturers not to be involved with a western company. General Motors (GM), Ford and Chrysler had shareholdings in Isuzu, Mazda and Mitsubishi respectively. Was Honda already looking elsewhere? British Leyland could not afford to miss another opportunity. We subsequently discovered that our concern was unnecessary, as the independent-minded Honda was not actively seeking a collaborative partner.

From the moment that the decision was made to approach Honda, things went the right way. Michael Edwardes knew Sir Fred Warner, a retired ambassador to Japan, who was on the Chloride Board and who was also a Director of Guinness Peat. He decided to approach Honda through Sir Fred, whose position as a former ambassador provided excellent credentials. Sir Fred and Mr Kiyoshi Kawashima (then President of Honda) met in Tokyo in September 1978.

At this meeting, the message was conveyed that the British Leyland Board believed there to be areas of mutual interest which could merit discussion between the companies. This message was received in a polite but guarded fashion by Mr Kawashima. He explained that Honda's tradition was one of independence, however he did believe that the British Leyland initiative required serious consideration. He would discuss the idea with a small group of his colleagues and then communicate with Sir Fred. These discussions took place and, to our relief, by late September communications were established with Mr Kiyoshi Ikemi, Deputy General Manager of the International Planning Office, and arrangements were being made for a meeting between a small group of executives from both companies. In the speed of this response Honda again confounded the perceived understanding of Japanese companies which was that, on major issues, it took them a long time and a lot of internal review and consensus-reaching to come to a decision. Because of this normally justified perception, we had been concerned that Mr Kawashima's first response to Sir Fred might have been a polite way of avoiding saying "no" to a distinguished visitor or, at least, the start of a very lengthy internal discussion within Honda. Not so; by early October, the arrangements were in hand for a group of three from each company to meet in San Francisco at the end of the month.

San Francisco was chosen on the basis that it was roughly halfway for each group and also because it was totally neutral territory and thus safe from the security viewpoint. The British Leyland group comprised David Andrews, Ray Horrocks (who had recently joined the company as Managing Director of Austin Morris) and myself. The Honda team included Mr Noboru Okamura (Senior Managing Director), Mr Masami Suzuki (Managing Director) and Mr Kiyoshi Ikemi. There was no formal agenda agreed in advance. The purpose of the meeting was to have an exchange of views, with the object of establishing whether sufficient common ground existed to justify exploring some form of collaboration. We were to stay at the Fairmont Hotel and it was agreed that the meetings, for which two days were allocated, would be held there.

British Leyland was very keen to see a broad range of collaboration agreed in principle. Before our departure, David arranged a pre-meeting to review the briefing document which I had prepared, and also to agree how we would handle the meeting. We were all ex-Ford and knew one another well, which made relationships easy. This was 1978 and far more of us smoked in those days than now. David was a non-smoker, Ray mainly smoked my cigarettes, and I was a serious smoker. At the end of the pre-meeting Ray, emphasising the wish to have the meetings go as smoothly as possible, suggested that, if the Honda team proved to be non-smokers, I should desist. It is a measure of my wish to see a constructive outcome that I readily agreed to make this major sacrifice!

We had a suite at the Fairmont with a large sitting room which was to be used as the meeting room. At 10.00 am on 27 October there was a knock on the door. I opened it and in came the three gentlemen who we were to get to know very well in the future. The introductions were made, business cards exchanged and we got under way. To my great amusement (and relief), as they sat down each of the Honda team formally placed his cigarettes and lighter on the table in front of him. All except Kiyoshi Ikemi that is. He added pipe, tobacco pouch, pipe reamer and matches to his pile! I knew that I had fallen among friends, produced my Marlborough and lighter, winked at Ray and the meeting started. (To make this narrative more acceptable in today's world it should be recorded that both Kiyoshi and I have now been 'failed' smokers for some years). The meeting proceeded in a relaxed fashion with Kiyoshi Ikemi acting as interpreter, a role he was to fill at many subsequent senior management meetings, in addition to his important operational role in the relationship.

The British Leyland team explained their view of the way in which the industry would develop, with emphasis on the potentially dangerous exposure of the smaller companies which could be overcome by sensible collaboration. The Honda team were non-committal, they asked questions about British Leyland's operations, about how the government ownership worked and about any existing collaborative relationships. They were very interested in our manufacturing activities on the continent, particularly the Seneffe assembly plant in Belgium.

The parties separated for lunch. The British Leyland team felt that the morning had gone well, however we were doing most of the talking with Honda being generally reactive and asking questions of fact. At this stage it was difficult to assess whether there was any potential for a successful outcome. Despite Mr Kawashima's speedy initial response we were concerned that we could be embarking on very lengthy discussions which might lead nowhere in the end. All our briefing from experts on Japan had stressed that a Japanese company would take a long time to make up its mind about such an idea.

When the meeting reconvened after lunch, we had planned to develop the case for collaboration further, leaving them with some ideas of possible areas of activity to consider overnight. We thus started to develop the case further without making specific proposals and then asked if they had any comments at this time. Their response surprised us somewhat. They agreed with our general conclusions about the future and the case for collaboration in theory and so they had a proposal to make – would British Leyland consider building a new car which Honda were developing? After what had seemed a rather non-committal attitude until then, this proposal was quite unexpected. We certainly expressed our willingness to hear them out. They explained that they believed that a collaborative relationship had to develop on a step-by-step basis. It was necessary to establish whether or not we could work together effectively. In their view, the best way to do this was to have a joint project as a test. Their specific proposal was that British Leyland should build, from components supplied by Honda to the Seneffe assembly plant in Belgium, this new family car which they had under development. They would then sell it in the European Economic Community (EEC) markets badged as a British Leyland car. Then came the difficulty: only if we agreed in principle would they tomorrow give us more details of the product.

We now had a problem. Although the proposition might be of interest, dependent on what the product was, British Leyland really wanted a broadly based collaboration and Honda was not prepared to commit to that at this stage. Equally they wouldn't release any details of the product unless we said that we were genuinely interested. It was a polite but definite stand-off. We met again the following morning and the discussion continued but only moved forward slightly. The Honda team clarified their proposal to the extent that the car was identified as being between Civic and Accord. They also explained that their proposal that the vehicle be built at Seneffe was made because they thought that it would be the simplest route for us, as Seneffe was used to building from what were known as Complete-Knock-Down (CKD) kits. This was in fact a very logical approach. What we could not tell them was that, for us, the only question about Seneffe was when and how we would divest ourselves of it. The clarification that they were not for some reason insisting on Seneffe as the production source was a small help.

We could not, however, proceed any further until David had consulted Michael Edwardes and the Board. We parted amicably, agreeing that we would review the position in the UK and respond to them by the end of November. We did agree that, if the response was positive, we would have another meeting in January. Another thing which was agreed was to maintain secrecy; knowledge of the discussions would be closely contained on an absolute 'need to know' basis. We were particularly concerned about security at this time, as British Leyland was always newsworthy and was extremely leaky, probably as a result of the major internal upheavals which were taking place.

We returned to the UK and a period of uncertainty followed. From my personal point of view, I did believe that we should grasp the nettle and go ahead with Honda. I recognised the fundamental need for a relationship of strategic significance but genuinely believed that we should gamble on Honda. At the time I had the impression, rightly or wrongly, that the Board were not united in their support for a Japanese relationship. During this period, I was in communication with Kiyoshi Ikemi, trying to convince Honda to make some move to indicate a warmness to the concept of a broader, long-term relationship. Eventually, without any significant clarification of the situation either way it was agreed that the January meeting should go ahead in Japan and that we would be given more information about the car. Fortunately, this time, as so often in the future, both companies took a pragmatic approach, kept talking, and a way was found.

It was a new team that left for Tokyo in late January. It was led by Mike Carver, British Leyland's Director of Strategic Planning, with Mark Snowdon, then Austin Morris Product Planning Director, and myself. Again, we were all ex-Ford and knew one another well. Mike and I had joined British Leyland at about the same time, he direct from Ford, me from Chrysler-Rootes. Mark was the youngest of the three of us and had originally been recruited by Mike. We all got on well enough to be able to argue without subsequent rancour, a very important element in a team, but one which isn't always easy to achieve. Sir Fred Warner met us in Tokyo and carried out the introductions, thus formally confirming our credentials.

My detailed recollection of this trip is less clear, the jetlag and the horrendous journey from Narita Airport into central Tokyo definitely got to my memory cells. My old passport tells me that we were there from 28 January to 1 February. We stayed at the Okura Hotel, which became the favourite for the early days of the relationship. The main meetings were held at the Palace Hotel, which was Honda's choice for a discreet meeting place. We were given details of the car at last and taken into an obscure corner of Wako, which was then Honda's Research and Development (R&D) base, to be shown a model of the car. It turned out to be a 4-door notchback, a new Civic derivative being developed for the Japanese market. The configuration was a disappointment as we had previously managed to convince ourselves that it would be a 5-door hatchback, which was desperately needed in the Austin Morris range. Our thinking had been that a suitable hatchback could have replaced the ageing Allegro some two years before the Maestro became available.

To recap on the new structure introduced by Michael Edwardes (mentioned earlier), it is desirable to pause at this point and briefly explain the status of British Leyland's car organisation and product strategy in 1979. There were now three groups; Austin Morris and Jaguar Rover Triumph were responsible for the design, development and manufacture of their respective model ranges; British Leyland Europe and Overseas was responsible for sales. There were product problems in both car groups, the most pressing of which were seen to be in Austin Morris. There had been no significant new product in the volume car range since the 1975 launch of the 18-22 Series (subsequently renamed the Princess). The vitally important mid-range sector would have to continue to be covered by the now aged Austin Maxi, Morris Marina and Austin Allegro, supported by the equally aged Triumph Dolomite from Jaguar Rover Triumph. The Metro would not arrive until 1980. The Maestro and Montego were not due until 1983-84.

As the 4-door Accord covered the Montego market segment, and we were told that the car being offered by Honda was 'between the Civic and Accord', we hoped that the car might provide a more speedily achievable alternative to Maestro. It was probably wishful thinking on our part. It should also be remembered that, at this stage, British Leyland was also considering other collaborative possibilities as a fall-back should the Honda discussions not come to a satisfactory conclusion. Against this background the revelation that the car was a booted saloon rather than a 5-door hatchback came as both a shock and a disappointment.

There was much discussion and midnight oil burning at the Okura Hotel which resulted in the case being developed for the vehicle to replace the Dolomite in the Jaguar Rover Triumph range, rather than going to Austin Morris. There were no plans at this time for a Dolomite replacement. There was a lot of telephoning to the UK and we produced an outline report on how we believed it could all work. We all departed, having promised to advise Honda formally of British Leyland's position. Mike Carver returned via Frankfurt, where he had arranged to meet Michael Edwardes to give him personal feedback.

Sir Fred Warner also had a meeting with Mr Kawashima who expressed pleasure at the way in which the talks had progressed and sent the message that he saw this first project as a test for both companies; if it worked to our mutual satisfaction further developments of the relationship were probable. The British Leyland Board accepted the recommendation that we should proceed with discussions and negotiations. Overall responsibility was assigned to Mike Carver, assisted by myself. Pratt Thompson, the Managing Director of Jaguar Rover Triumph, had confidence that we would take care of his interests.

It should be noted that, at this stage, the emphasis was on closing the product gap, with some feeling that there might be some ideas on manufacturing efficiency to pick up, although it was felt that the cultural differences would make this difficult. In some areas of the company there was a reluctance to accept that there was a serious quality problem and a belief that, even if there was one, it was caused by bad industrial relations with the workers on the track, and anyway it would be solved by the new models when they came. Despite all evidence to the contrary, this attitude remained in place for several years and certainly reduced substantially the benefit which British Leyland could have gained from the relationship with Honda in the first half of the 1980s. Michael Edwardes was conscious of the problem but the real causes remained unacknowledged for a long time. It is fair to say that those who had a direct involvement in the markets outside the UK started off with a much clearer appreciation of our quality inadequacies and the enormous quality superiority of the Japanese products at that time. The attitude in the UK was still that Japanese cars were mainly successful because they were low priced and offered a lot of features for the money.

After the decision to continue positively with the discussions was made, it was agreed that a joint press release should be issued. The British Leyland side was particularly keen to avoid the possibility of a leak taking place. In addition, there was a good story to put across about the 'new British Leyland' with the chance to emphasise the positive aspects of a Japanese relationship to minimise the effect of any 'anti' attitudes. In late March John Mackay, British Leyland's Director of Communications, and I flew out to Tokyo to agree the line which the two companies would take in their press releases and in any subsequent discussions with the media. The meetings went smoothly and constructively. The press announcement was made on 3 April 1979 and was generally well received in the UK.

Looking back after 16 years of the relationship with Honda, and now that Honda, Nissan and Toyota are all established with their own UK manufacturing operations, it is difficult to appreciate the justifiable nervousness which was felt about announcing the link with a Japanese manufacturer. There was, at that time, the risk of very vocal opposition in the UK, although happily this did not arise. The major adverse reactions to the announcement came from within the industry; the most vocal from Nissan and Renault, both of whom had earlier connections with the company.

The Nissan connection went back a long way. The first Datsun car in the 1930s was based on the Austin Seven and, as it was not a licensed product, Sir Herbert Austin had one brought to the UK to check whether it infringed any of his patents. Evidently it did not and the matter rested. There was, however, a follow-up as, after the war, Nissan did become a licensed assembler of CKD Austins, and derivatives of the B-Series power unit lived on in the Nissan engine range until the 1980s. There had also been a very brief discussion between the companies on possible engine supply in about 1977, but this had not come to anything. They were evidently outraged that we had not gone to them if we wanted a Japanese partner and, allegedly, they went to the British Embassy in Tokyo to register a complaint.

As mentioned earlier, there had also been some lengthy discussions with Renault. These were terminated quite specifically by David Andrews at a meeting with the then head of Renault's car operations, Bernard Hanon (at which I was present) well before the Honda discussions got under way. Nevertheless, Renault was vociferous in its objection to the news and was quoted in the press claiming that we were still in substantial discussions with themselves.

There were some lighter aspects of the trip to Tokyo with John Mackay. At that time there were two main routes, the Polar route via Anchorage and the Moscow route over Russia. Despite being shorter, Moscow was less popular because a) the Russians would not allow wide-bodied airliners to use the route, which meant that fairly aged Boeing 707s were the norm, and b) it meant a break in the transit lounge of the old Moscow Airport, which was high on everyone's list of least entertaining ways of spending an hour or two. Because of the timing of the flight, for this trip we went out via Moscow. In the transit lounge we decided to pass the time by having a beer in the cafe. The intercom system was virtually inaudible and so we did not hear our flight being called. Suddenly a figure appeared at our table: "were we Messrs McKay and Bacchus?" We were to: "please come quickly the flight is waiting." Faced with the possibility of being marooned in Moscow we picked up our briefcases and ran. As we got to the exit we were confronted by an awe-inspiring vision - "STOP!" it bellowed (in English, to be fair). We stopped and were confronted by the original model for *Giles* the cartoonist's female Russian soldier. She was about five feet high, at least that wide, in ankle length greatcoat and boots, and clutching a Kalashnikov which was pointed vaguely in our direction. I'm sure that we looked just like two small boys caught scrumping apples. She pointed at our cases, we opened them with alacrity and then, released, leapt onto the waiting bus with considerable relief.

The rest of the journey was uneventful. When we arrived at the hotel (the Okura again) John suggested a Japanese meal. We had a pleasant evening interrupted by the type of flavour shock which can be a feature of life for the unwary eater in Japan. Halfway through the meal a sorbet arrived, a green sorbet; good, I thought, it must be lime from the colour. I took a spoonful. It wasn't lime, it was green tea sorbet! Green tea is very much an acquired taste. After 88 trips to Japan I have managed to achieve a tolerance of, but not a taste for it. Unless one is an addict, green tea sorbet is definitely best avoided, particularly if one is expecting a refreshing, astringent citrus taste.

Labour Prime Minister Harold Wilson visits the Solihull factory. He was the architect of the merger which created BLMC in 1968

Future Conservative Prime Minister Margaret Thatcher visits the Cowley factory. She would be rather less enthusiastic about owning a car company.

Michael Edwardes, Chairman of British Leyland 1977-82. Famous for battling the trade unions and extensively restructuring the company.

Kiyoshi Kawashima, Honda President 1973-83. He established the partnership with British Leyland.

David Andrews, Finance Director, British Leyland

Mark Snowdon, Managing Director, Austin Rover

Harold Musgrove, Chairman, Austin Rover

Chapter 4
1979: BOUNTY IS LAUNCHED
No, it's not a chocolate bar, it's a car!

The next step was to get the commercial parameters of the project identified to the furthest extent possible, and also to get the plans for the physical delivery of the project underway. The project acquired the code name 'Bounty' at this time. In these early stages of the relationship, we frequently used the Stafford Hotel in St James' Place in London for meetings and entertaining. We were having a small meeting with the senior Honda team and Pratt Thompson was there in his role as Managing Director of Jaguar Rover Triumph. I was called out to take what turned out to be a lengthy phone call; on returning, it was to discover that Pratt had suggested the code name 'Bounty' and this had been agreed. As an American Pratt had, quite justifiably, thought of the word in its dictionary definition. Needless to say, it took a little while for internal derisory comments about chocolate coated coconut bars to settle down. Pratt had the last laugh, the project turned out to conform to his interpretation of the name. There were no mutinies either!

By this time, it had been decided that the vehicle would be badged as a Triumph and it would be built at the Canley factory in Coventry, with the body produced at the Speke plant near Liverpool. Honda took some convincing on the latter point. The idea of shipping a completed body from Liverpool to Coventry struck them as a little strange. They were right, it wasn't really desirable. For historic reasons, however, British Leyland did quite a lot of it, particularly Jaguar Rover Triumph. They did come to accept the fact of it if not the logic.

April was a very busy month, with important visits by Honda to Europe and British Leyland to Japan. Early in the month, very shortly after the press announcement, we received the first visit in strength. This was significant, as the first opportunity for us to get to know three gentlemen who played key roles in the project and two of whom went on to become key figures in the development of the wider relationship. These were Mr Tetsuo Chino, Mr Fujio Ishikawa and Mr Shuko Hayashi.

Messrs Chino and Ishikawa were both members of the Honda Board, Mr Chino was a commercial man and Mr Ishikawa a manufacturing engineer. They were responsible for the delivery of the commercial and technical aspects respectively of the project. Shuko Hayashi was at this time a Manager in the Honda International Planning Office, a colleague of Kiyoshi Ikemi. He remained deeply involved with the relationship throughout and by 1989 was stationed at Honda's European headquarters in Reading with the position of Director, Rover Liaison. Mr Chino carried through all the commercial negotiations on the project and then went off to play a major role in the continued development of Honda's US operations. Mr Ishikawa remained a key player in the relationship and contributed a great amount to it until he retired in the late 1980s, having risen to become an Executive Vice-President of Honda.

A large Honda team arrived at Seneffe for a quick visit, which was followed by a speedy transfer to the UK and visits to Speke, Canley and Solihull. These visits were critically important as they would be Honda's first exposure to the facilities which we intended to use for Bounty. Neither Speke nor Canley was regarded as a jewel in British Leyland's manufacturing crown and there was a degree of nervousness about the reaction to the tour. The Solihull plant had recently been the subject of major expenditure for expansion and modernisation to launch the Rover SD1. It was felt that it should be included to demonstrate that we did have a state of the art plant. I didn't think it a good idea because I was concerned that, once they had seen the Solihull facilities, they would try to persuade us to use them for Bounty. In the event we were all wrong. Mr Ishikawa declared himself quite happy that the job could be done as planned. He also, informally, told me that he was not terribly impressed by Solihull and thought that it was not particularly efficient!

During this visit the first serious discussions were held to define the level of local content which the vehicle would have at the start of production. The key decision made at this time was that the body would be locally sourced from the start. It was also agreed that there would be a very quick follow up visit to Japan for the key people in Jaguar Rover Triumph who would be involved in the technical aspects of the project so that they could gain an understanding of the way Honda would be carrying out their end of the project. What we were embarked upon was new to both companies and there was a lot of learning to do if it was to move swiftly and smoothly ahead.

The arrangements were made, the plan being for me to accompany the group for the main part of their visit but then to leave them and meet Mike Carver in Tokyo for commercial and strategic discussions with the Honda Headquarters team. In the event, due to my other commitments, it was agreed that the team, which was mainly senior production engineers, would go out on their own and I would join them at their first port of call which was Suzuka, Honda's small car plant. During the last couple of days before the team left, I was in Brussels on business and I arrived home in the evening prior to them leaving for Japan the next day. There was a phone call from Pratt Thompson to tell me that it had been decided to include in the party the Canley Works Convenor, Eddie McGarry. The idea was that Eddie, who was a well-known and vocal trade union representative, should see for himself how Honda worked and thus, hopefully, avoid any ill-informed union opposition to the project. In the circumstances of 1979 this news came as a surprise to me, however Honda had agreed and the team were on their way. It all worked very well, the team got on well together, with Eddie an integral part of it, and there were certainly no subsequent union problems related to the originally proposed project at Canley.

Whilst in Brussels I had met with Mr Nakajima, who was then Honda's representative there, and who had attended some of the technical meetings. It was an excellent opportunity to establish contact with Honda on a slightly less formal basis, and also provided an easier communication link in those pre-fax days. We had a useful discussion and he imparted the message (off the record) that Honda was encouraged by the way in which things were progressing and by British Leyland's enthusiasm for the project. There was surprise at the high level of investment which we considered to be necessary and also at the absence of engineers from the British Leyland senior management group. I did pass these messages on, the latter point in particular echoed a longstanding concern of my own. The messages sank without trace, but it is right to record that the eventual investment bill for Bounty provided much more for the money than was envisaged at this early stage.

I joined the team at Suzuka, everything went well and we were impressed by the efficiency and orderliness of the Honda operation, which was a marked contrast to the standards in our own plants at that time. The team then left to visit the Sayama plant, whilst I moved on to Tokyo to join Mike Carver and Rod Turner (Jaguar Rover Triumph Controller) for commercial discussions.

This round of meetings was very significant. As well as providing the outline cost parameters for the vehicle, we had the first discussions about the tooling programmes which would be required to provide the locally sourced panels. Another important part of the discussions concerned a draft Memorandum of Understanding about the project, which was intended to provide protection for both parties due to the need for all the preparations to continue whilst the contractual negotiations went on. One aspect of the Memorandum of Understanding was a commitment by both parties to work to have the Agreement signed by the end of the year. At this stage Mike and I did not regard the achievement of this timing objective as a problem. How wrong we were this story will show. The Memorandum of Understanding, however, was not a problem and Mike Carver and Mr Okamura signed it in mid-May. It was the easiest agreement that we ever concluded and, unlike its successors, caused hardly any argument!

Another notable aspect of this meeting was that it introduced us to Honda's UK-based lawyers, Freshfields. Over the years of the relationship, they remained an important part of the British Leyland/Rover-Honda team, with us using our in-house legal advisors. Tribute should be paid to Freshfields for the very constructive role which they played throughout the relationship and in particular to Nick Spearing, who joined when he was still a junior, acting as Honda's legal advisor, and who would become a senior partner. While always representing his client's interests he was always constructive in his approach and gained the unanimous respect of those of us in regular contact and negotiation with him. During the visit, armed with the preliminary information from Honda, the three of us were able to put together the financial outlines of the project, sufficient to indicate that it could be profitable. This was further refined on our return and happily we were given the ok to continue, and thus the Memorandum of Understanding could be signed.

We really did believe at this stage that we could clear the Agreement by the end of September. The timing pressure was there as, quite apart from our urgent need for product, Honda was pressing quite firmly that we should start production no more than twelve months after they started in Japan. This gave us just over two years to get into production, by the standards of those days a worryingly short time. If the timing was to be met, the long lead funds would need to be committed quite soon. The complication was that the overall funding would have to be approved by the Department of Trade and Industry - who represented our major shareholder - as a part of the Corporate Plan which was due later in the year.

The discussions, negotiations and preparations continued through May, June and July. They went well, the companies showed positive signs of being able to work together constructively. Behind the scenes in British Leyland however there were great problems – with the company, not the Honda relationship. The terrible combination of high inflation and a strengthening pound sterling was creating havoc with British Leyland's precarious hold on viability. The events of that summer are set out in detail in Sir Michael Edwardes' book *Back from the Brink*, which gives the story right from the horse's mouth. As far as this account is concerned, the critical results were the decision to close Speke and the manufacturing facilities at Canley, coupled with the certainty that the approval of the 1980 Corporate Plan by the new Conservative Government would be an even more difficult problem than usual.

We had a product (hopefully) but nowhere to build it. The partner was pressing on at his end, blissfully unaware of this, as were most people, it being a closely guarded secret within British Leyland. The management were determined to keep the project alive and so a plan was quickly hatched to build the car at Cowley, even though it was to remain badged a Triumph, and Cowley was an Austin Morris plant.

Chapter 5
1979/80: A CHANGE OF DIRECTION
At least the car and the name remain the same

The internal decision had been made, now the news had to be conveyed to the partner. There was a degree of concern about this. We had spent some time convincing Honda of the logic of the Canley/Speke/Jaguar Rover Triumph route; now we intended to move to Cowley/Austin Morris and preserve the timing. The physical change was difficult enough; however the reason behind it was the major concern. We were beginning to get the message that Honda was already feeling comfortable with the relationship, which was important to British Leyland's need for long term collaboration. Having to now convey the message of organisational and physical restructuring made for quite a challenge. The proposed new plan was defined in a little more detail, sufficient to explain it convincingly, in particular to Mr Suzuki and Mr Ishikawa. The background to it was, however, that we were committed to signing the Agreement by the end of the year and starting production by mid-1981, less than two years away. This was combined with serious concerns about constructing a Corporate Plan acceptable to the new Conservative Government led by Margaret Thatcher. Even with Michael Edwardes in charge, British Leyland as an operation was very low down on Mrs Thatcher's popularity chart.

The trip to Tokyo was arranged, Mike Carver and I arrived at Narita Airport (according to my old passport) on 5 August and departed again on 9 August. We stayed at the Okura, which was by then becoming a home from home, and prepared ourselves for the meeting on the 6 August. The meeting took place in the morning and was not comfortable. The Honda team was led by Mr Okamura and Mr Suzuki, they heard the explanations and the outline of the revised plan, asked a few questions for clarification, and then asked for time to think about the implications for them. We went back to the hotel, had some lunch and received a message that they would call us the following morning as they wanted the rest of the day, at least, to discuss the situation internally. It was very much a 'don't call us, we'll call you' situation and we were left with the distinct impression that they had problems with the change of plan. It was not a relaxed afternoon and evening but there was nothing to do but wait and develop plans for, hopefully, the urgent next steps for the new project. The call came the following day and they announced that they wanted to discuss the matter further. We went off to the meeting with some trepidation but when we started they announced that they did not have any fundamental objections. We were able to satisfy their questions and to develop the new plan with them. Plans were also agreed for a speedy follow up meeting with the Austin Morris management to get the operational aspects of the project underway.

The project brought more benefits to Cowley than just the model. It brought with it a new, very large, automated press line (the first in the company) and the new 'AB' paint plant. There was, however, a sacrifice to be made. To provide the funding required to support the project it was decided to drop a programme then in the early stages of development codenamed AM1. This was a 2-door, booted version of the Metro. Later on, a 5-door Metro was brought into the range which proved far more marketable than the 2-door would have been, so the sacrifice was very well worthwhile.

Once the new plan was put in place we continued with the contractual negotiations. These were undoubtedly the easiest which we had over all the ensuing years. This was because both parties were keen to see the deal done amicably, and the strategic responsibility was held centrally in British Leyland. In addition, we did not have the benefit of actual operating experience (which we would have in future) to provide a problem checklist to address.

The greatest concern was whether there was anything in the Agreement to which the European Commission would take exception. Both companies wanted to see the car sold throughout the European Economic Community (EEC) and in those days Community Law was far less understood than now. The simple solution of course was to show them a copy of the draft and ask for their comments. We tried that. The official response from the Directorate-General responsible for scrutinising fair competition was that they could only review signed, completed agreements. By the time we reached that stage it would be too late! To be fair to the much-maligned bureaucrats, they were actually very helpful and, although refusing to look at any document, they were prepared to comment orally on ideas which we put to them in the same way. We did not appear to have any serious problems, as far as we could tell, and so we went ahead. It was not until shortly before we stopped production of the car that we received formal confirmation that the Agreement was acceptable.

In the October it was necessary to re-run the engineers' visit but this time with the new Austin Morris/Cowley team. This all went well but did not, this time, include a trade union representative. One of the memories of this trip was the journey back from Suzuka to Tokyo. We became typhoon bound on the Shinkansen (the Bullet Train), the overhead power lines having been brought down. We were a large group and many of the Austin Morris team had with them their duty-free liquor allowance, acquired on the journey out from the UK. After being marooned for some time, these bottles were opened, the waiting became less frustrating and a convivial party ensued, with our Honda colleagues joining in with enthusiasm. One of my clearest memories is of Mr Hori, a senior Honda manufacturing engineer involved in the project, drinking with enthusiasm a cocktail of Scotch and Campari; he offered some to me but I chickened out. The company's interests were vitally important, but one had to draw the line somewhere! By the time we eventually reached Tokyo Central Station, Mr Hori was very happy indeed. When we met the following morning, I asked him how he felt, anticipating that the quantity and mixture of the intake on the train should have guaranteed a world class hangover. To my disgust he responded that he felt fine and had thoroughly enjoyed the journey despite the delay. As he carried on being cheerful, I had to accept that it was his metabolism that was world class.

The Agreement was effectively finalised by this time and the programme for the project had received internal approval. However, the entire thing was bound up with the overall approval of the Corporate Plan by the Government. This turned out to be a lengthy process and our commitment to sign the Agreement by the end of the year was looking at risk. It was a tense situation all round; we were both pressing ahead physically with the project, based upon the Memorandum of Understanding, but the need for major financial commitment on both sides was getting close. The Government stated by early December that a decision would be made before Christmas, although what it would be was another question entirely. The Department of Trade and Industry was basically in favour of the Honda relationship, however it was the total Corporate Plan which the Government had to approve and the Bounty project was only a small part of that. It was decided that I should go out to Tokyo to be on the spot to convey messages and help ease the way if there should be any problems. It was undoubtedly one of the more miserable experiences, the problem being stress combined with boredom. I spent the first day with Honda discussing operational details on the project; however, at that time, apart from the fundamental issue of whether or not we would be able to go ahead, things were going fairly smoothly.

After the first day, we really didn't have anything we needed to talk about. The position in the UK was that a message could come through at almost any hour and therefore I needed to be close to the hotel and means of communication at all times. I was staying at the Imperial Hotel for that reason, which was close to the Ginza and Hibiya Park, and meant that I could more easily slip out for fresh air, exercise and window shopping during the least likely communication hours. Nevertheless, I couldn't stray far. The Imperial is one of the world's great hotels and I have stayed there many times over the years, however I have never developed an affection for it, having had a surfeit of it in December 1979.

Eventually the message came through, the Government had approved the Corporate Plan, and so the signing could go ahead. By this time, we were very close to Christmas and Honda were to start their New Year holiday three or four days later. There didn't seem to be much time for a signing ceremony. Mike then called to say that he was coming over on Christmas Eve and that Michael Edwardes and John McKay were leaving on Christmas Day. The signing was planned for 27 December in Tokyo and it would be left up to me whether I stayed or not. If I stayed, they would bring my wife out with them. As we had a young family and Christmas arrangements which involved other people, I decided to return home, having confirmed arrangements with Honda.

I therefore missed the historic event which took place on my birthday and, regretfully, the opportunity to meet Mr Honda himself, who joined the group after the signing ceremony. I still have the inscribed Mont Blanc fountain pen which was used for the signing and a very clever Seiko watch which tells the correct time for anywhere in the world at the touch of a button. This is pretty ordinary stuff now, but in 1979 it was a miracle of technology.

Mike Carver had useful discussions with the Honda team during the visit which indicated that they were likely to be receptive to further ideas on collaboration. It appeared that the gamble which the British Leyland Board took in deciding to go for collaboration with Honda, without a clear position on the ongoing potential being established, had been justified. As had been intended, the Christmas Day departure from the UK received the maximum media coverage and the follow up comments in the press were generally guardedly favourable. We were now absolutely committed to go ahead, with production due to start in 18 months' time. The responsibility for the delivery of the project was assigned to Mike Fernyhough who was then in charge of the Southern Operations of Austin Morris. Supported by a first-class team, Mike ran a textbook project control process and the combined efforts of Cowley and Honda delivered the project in an exemplary fashion.

The New Year saw a change of job for me. I left behind the Bounty project and the small team which had been providing splendid support for the last six months, and moved to be Director of Finance and Planning, Jaguar Rover Triumph. This was a relatively short-lived experience, as by the autumn Jaguar Rover Triumph was the subject of an internal takeover by Austin Morris, the combination being initially referred to as Light Medium Cars. I moved back into that organisation and so came back into direct communication with Honda and the members of my old Bounty team again.

During 1980, there were ongoing discussions on strategy, and a working group was set up to explore collaborative possibilities of all sorts. The impression which I had at this time was that there was more enthusiasm for a long-term relationship from the British Leyland Board, which was at the centre, than in Austin Morris, whose attitude was, and remained for a long time, that they could do all that was necessary themselves, given a bit of short-term support with Honda product like Bounty. This situation existed through to the middle of the decade, and resulted in the failure to seize the opportunity to learn from Honda, which was not only available but was also being enthusiastically offered.

Honda itself was not reluctant to learn; at this time, it did very little car CKD business. British Leyland on the other hand had many years of experience in the art of pack-planning or fitting the bits into the boxes in the most space effective way. Honda was very open at the time about how much it had learned on the subject from Austin Morris. Given that by 1996 they were building about a million cars a year outside Japan, it was a very useful secondary benefit to them.

The company, and particularly Austin Morris, was extremely busy in 1980 launching the Metro, which was done with great success both for the product and for the image of British Leyland as a whole. It did mean that there weren't any major developments on the Honda front, basically everyone just got on with the Bounty project. I always believed that Mike Fernyhough and the project team were assisted in their efforts by the fact that the rest of the Austin Morris management was totally immersed in Metro and the industrial relations scene, thus they left an excellent team alone to get on and do the right thing.

1980 did feature other developments. I was involved in discussions with BMW on possible collaboration with Jaguar Rover Triumph. Although these came to nothing (until 1994) the experience did impress me with one thing, the similarity between BMW and Honda. Neither would agree with this but to an interested observer it is so. They are both engineers' companies; they are both primarily engine manufacturers and are very good at it; they are both into motorbikes; and their technical self-confidence verges on arrogance. They are also both pretty successful although relatively small on the world scale.

Honda began the manufacture of motorbikes in 1946. Their breakthrough motor car was the Honda Civic of 1972. From December 1973 it was offered with Honda's newly developed CVCC low-emission engine.

The Honda Civic was also successful overseas. This early publicity shot from 1974 shows it in a very 'English' setting in London.

British Leyland's model range was overblown with vehicles which were well designed but did not fulfil their potential. The Rover SD1, for example, was attractive but unreliable. This early example is being examined on a test rig in 1977.

New models were on the way. This is LM11, which would become the Austin Montego, in the Longbridge Design Studio circa 1980; but British Leyland needed a new product sooner than its existing programme could deliver.

On 27 December 1979, Michael Edwardes and Kyoshi Kawashima met in Tokyo to sign the Agreement which marked the beginning of the British Leyland/Honda partnership. The pen (which Edwardes is holding in his left hand) was later given to John Bacchus, to be kept as a memento of this landmark event.

The completed Triumph Acclaim on view at Longbridge. The plaque on the floor records the date as 19 February 1981.

Harold Musgrove, Managing Director of Austin Morris/Austin Rover, in front of the Triumph Acclaim automatic framing jig on the Cowley body assembly line at the start of production in 1981.

Cowley had received a multi-million pound investment to update its facilities for Acclaim production, including a new paint shop.

A new technique was introduced from Honda for the installation of the engine. Instead of the body being dropped onto the power unit from overhead, the drivetrain was lifted up into the body using an hydraulic ram table. This made assembly easier and also reduced the risk of damage. Known as 'stuff-up' this method would become standard in British Leyland's factories.

As they reached the end of the line, the fully assembled vehicles underwent a final inspection and polish to ready them for dispatch.

The Triumph Acclaim was not the most exciting car visually, and had only one engine size, but it was a great achievement in a short space of time. It convinced both partners that they could work together and that the venture was worth continuing.

The next stage in the relationship was the 'XX' project. The formal agreement to proceed was signed in November 1981 in Tokyo. Here the two parties are exchanging gifts after the event. Far left is Honda President Mr Kawashima, Mr Sakuma and Ray Horrocks are shaking hands, John Bacchus is on the right.

A press conference was held after the signing. On the left are John Bacchus and Andy Barr, in the centre, addressing journalists, is Mark Snowdon, and on the right are Ray Horrocks, President Kawashima and Mr Okamura.

In John's words 'It hadn't been easy …'

Chapter 6
1981: AN EVENTFUL YEAR
This could be the start of something big

As the 1980s proceeded, there were more reorganisations within the company and Austin Rover Group Ltd (which I will refer to as Austin Rover) emerged as the central player.

In the first few months of 1981, I was involved in the Bounty delivery process and was only peripherally aware that there seemed to be some upset with Honda at the corporate level. It appeared to soon blow over and, as it did not seem to be getting in the way of the delivery of Bounty, I didn't worry about it too much. It was only later in the year, on coming back into a role of involvement in the core aspects of the relationship, that I caught up with what had happened.

Very early in the year, a meeting had been held involving Michael Edwardes and Mr Kawashima together with some of their senior directors. The object of the meeting was to discuss the potential for further collaboration between the two companies. The depressed state of the markets, pressure from the Government, and the announcement of Nissan's intention to build a plant in the UK, all emphasised British Leyland's need to accelerate the sorting out of its car operations if it was to survive. The discussions were probably pretty wide ranging and may well have touched on the question of shareholding. Given the Government pressure for 'privatisation' it would be surprising if it had not been touched upon. The impression I subsequently gained was that, initially, British Leyland's senior management was pleased with the outcome of the meeting.

Things went wrong very quickly however. There was a press leak in Tokyo (source unknown) which led to Honda making statements to the press that it was considering equity participation in British Leyland. This all happened without any consultation with British Leyland and, quite understandably, caused considerable anger. Fortunately, for some reason the British media did not pick up the story to any significant degree, and so we were spared what could have turned into a very embarrassing and damaging public argument between the companies. After some sharp messages from the UK, some form of accommodation was reached and henceforth all public relations activities were carefully co-ordinated. Although there was the occasional problem – usually, it must be said, when a Honda individual spoke out of turn – it worked. Eventually things calmed down and, after a break in amicabilities, talking recommenced.

Things really got underway again with a meeting at the flat in Whitehall Court, London, owned by British Leyland. This event took place during the late spring or early summer between Michael Edwardes and Mr Kawashima. Here, the first steps were taken to set up what became the XX project. This very quickly gathered momentum and developed into what was, at that time, the most imaginative and complex project ever undertaken by two independent companies in the motor industry. It is necessary to provide an explanation of the background and outline of the project so that its significance can be put in perspective. The most apt subtitle for the XX project would be: 'this could be the start of something big'. It grew from the fertile soil of genuine need on the part of both partners. British Leyland needed a replacement for the Rover SD1, a classic, brilliant in concept but, as so often, deeply flawed in execution. Honda needed to move upmarket, most specifically in the USA where its sales were very rapidly expanding.

At this time, there was a project in the Corporate Plan for a replacement for the Austin Ambassador and Rover SD1, codenamed LM14/15. In broad principle, this involved stretching the LM11 platform (Montego) - which was itself a stretched LM10 platform (Maestro) - even further by extending the wheelbase and accommodating larger engines. It was not clearly defined, other than as a point on the timing chart and a financial provision in the plan. The concept was never really any more than an indication that something would have to be done. Honda R&D soon found that the fundamental technical aspects posed too great a challenge to proceed. One thing which was agreed from the beginning was that the car would be a transverse-engined, front-wheel drive layout. In 1981 this was a very advanced approach, and a brave one, as executive cars of that driveline layout were limited to the Citroen CX and the Austin Ambassador, and they had 4-cylinder engines only.

The early discussions in both the UK and Japan very quickly resulted in the definition of a project which was imaginative and extremely forward looking. The original concept was for a car which would be largely common but with clear identity differentials. Honda would provide a V6 power unit to be used in both versions, Austin Rover would provide its own 4-cylinder power unit, and both marque versions of the car would be built by each company. That is, Austin Rover would build both the Rover and Honda versions in Cowley and supply the Honda version to Honda for them to sell in Europe. Reciprocal arrangements would apply in Japan. The cars would be jointly designed and developed. It was a tribute to the management of both companies that they were prepared to embark on such an ambitious project when we had not yet launched the Acclaim into the market. These early stages went so well that we were ready to sign a Letter of Intent on the project by late November.

The signing of this document took place in Tokyo somewhat earlier than planned. I was out there and had agreed the final text of the document, the plan being that I would then return to the UK and, following formal Board consideration, a signing would take place. This was no problem as, throughout the years, once an action had been agreed by the negotiators, things carried on regardless of formal signatures. To my surprise I received a phone call from my boss, who by this time was Mark Snowdon, to say that it had been agreed that Ray Horrocks (now in charge of all car operations) and he were coming out to sign the document. I would stay on to make the arrangements with Honda, and be there for the ceremony and press conference. They had booked in at the New Otani Hotel from the UK. The change of plan was a surprise but not a problem; with a rapidly developing relationship underway there were always plenty of things which required my attention in Japan.

I decided to continue my stay at the Century Hyatt in Shinjuku, which had now become our regular hotel, being fairly close to Honda's then headquarters in Harajuku. On the day of their arrival, they were due in at about 4.00 pm. I finished my meeting with Honda at lunchtime and after lunch went straight to the New Otani to wait for them. On going to the reception desk to confirm that they were expected, I was told - "No!" By this time, they would have landed at Narita Airport if the flight was on time and, being JAL, it probably was. After a moment of consternation, sense took over. The New Otani was a huge hotel: "of course they had rooms for these unexpected guests?" "No!" was the response again. Hands full of Yen 100 coins, I started ringing the other hotels. They all claimed to be full. Returning to the reception desk, and with much arguing, I got through the first line of defence and finally reached the Duty Manager. When I explained the problem and emphasised that they were coming for a very important meeting with Mr Kawashima, the President of Honda, he magically produced three rooms from the Duty Manager's private stock. In the course of this process, we discovered the reason for the problem: the telex from the UK requesting the reservation said December not November! They were booked in, but one month later. We had only just sorted all this out when through the main doors came Ray and the rest of the party, smiling broadly because the flight had been early and the journey from Narita had been unusually quick. I did not tell them about the narrowly avoided disaster until later.

The signing ceremony was due to take place early the next morning, followed by a press conference. Arrangements for such things were always a problem because of the nine-hour time differential between London and Tokyo. We had agreed this one for an 8.00 am statement in Tokyo which meant 11.00 pm the previous evening in London. I was up early as I had to get to the New Otani where the activities were to take place. When my phone rang at about 6.30 am, I assumed that it was someone calling from the UK, but I was wrong. It was Kiyoshi Ikemi calling to say that Honda UK had been on the phone during the night to report that the announcement had been made during the evening on the BBC. We had somehow jumped the gun in London despite the agreed timetable and Mr Kawashima was not very happy. This has also to be seen in the context of the public relations upset earlier in the year when we had taken a very strong line with Honda. Fortunately, it was all sorted out quite quickly, with Ray apologising profusely to Mr Kawashima. I never did find out what had actually happened.

The overall result was good publicity for us both which was the important thing, particularly for British Leyland where it helped the slowly improving image of the company. The year also saw the public launch of the Triumph Acclaim, in October. All aspects of the launch went well. The motoring journalists were not overwhelmingly enthusiastic, by their standards it was not an exciting car. Sales did meet expectations, however, and the car was really left to sell itself after the initial launch publicity. What the car did do was to establish a very loyal and quietly enthusiastic owner body who thought very highly of their car, the company and the dealers. These were not the views generally held by the average British Leyland customer at that time.

The Acclaim challenged at least two views which were then firmly held within the company. The first of these was that a major contributor to the quality problem was the worker on the line. This was particularly true of the attitude to the Cowley workforce. In the event the Cowley people demonstrated that, if they were given something good to work with, then they would turn it into a high-quality product. The situation was neatly defined to me by one of the chaps on the final line, when I asked him how he found working on the Acclaim. His reply, as near verbatim as I can recall was: "Why don't our people design them like this? You have to be very determined to build it wrong." The truth of this message and its implications unfortunately took a long time to be accepted.

The second illusion to be broken was that, generally speaking, the dealers were not very good. This view appeared to be supported by market research findings which confirmed a low level of customer satisfaction with the dealers. After the Acclaim launch, we discovered a new situation. Not only were the customers very pleased with the car, but they also rated the dealers very highly. What was happening was that after buying the car, the customer's experience was limited to the scheduled servicing without the more usual list of recurring and frequently not fixable faults. The dealers demonstrated with the Acclaim that they could, given a product with the right level of quality and reliability, provide a high level of customer satisfaction.

On both counts the seeds of very important lessons were being sown but they were to have too long a germination period, even those which did not fall on stony ground. Shortly after the public launch a private celebration was held. Mike Carver arranged a dinner for the 'January 1979 Tokyo Team' and their wives. The Warners, Carvers, Snowdons and Bacchi had a very pleasant evening at the Stafford Hotel in London, which seemed to be a logical venue and anyway was excellent, as always. 1981 had proved to be an exciting and constructive year.

Chapter 7
1982: A BUSY YEAR
The start of the move to the 'Rover' brand

This was the year of getting the XX project seriously underway; it also saw the start of three other projects related to Japan which subsequently played important roles in the development of the company. These three were:

- The Acclaim replacement, which became the first Rover 200.
- The Honda PG1 transmission, which became widely used by Austin Rover Group.
- The formation of the company which was to become Rover Japan.

The XX project occupied most of the time however, and a great deal was happening.

The detailed story of the XX project deserves a book to itself and so this narrative will concentrate on the key elements as I recall them. Undoubtedly one significant factor was that we became aware of the emerging importance of Mr Tadashi Kume in the relationship. Mr Kume was at this time a Senior Managing Director of Honda and President of Honda R&D, and he took control of the project for Honda R&D. The remit was for a vehicle which was basically common in style but with clear identity differences.

The hard points of the basic dimensions were agreed quite quickly, and styling work got seriously underway. After a great deal of work in both companies, it became clear that a basically common style could not be agreed. One difficulty was that Honda needed the car to have a maximum width of 1700 mm, as this was then a significant tax break point in Japan. This did create some constraints but there were deeper disagreements around the theme of the style which caused the real problems. In essence Austin Rover wanted a car primarily for Europe, Honda wanted a car primarily for the USA. The corporate interpretations of these different market priorities were very different, and for a while it looked as though the project might founder on that particular rock.

A compromise was agreed, which was to have a common underbody with all the key welding points for the whole body also common. This made it feasible to build both bodies at both locations. It did mean, however, that there would not be as high a proportion of shared body tooling as had been originally planned. Much more importantly, it opened the door to the creeping reduction in commonality which meant that Austin Rover deprived itself of some of the major benefits which could have come from the project, and which would turn out to have very serious implications in the future.

Work continued in parallel in both companies; a project team was established within Austin Rover and I was, at this time, part of the Cars Group staff. My job included responsibility for the overall relationship with Honda and, in particular, ensuring that it stayed on the rails. The details of the project began to be hammered out, particularly between the product engineering groups in the two companies, where *hammered out* was frequently an accurate description of the process! Responsibility for the design and development of the common areas of the car was to be split on a system basis. Each company was to do its own identity engineering.

There were many problems which had to be resolved between the companies and the collision of conflicting engineering ideas was substantial. At this time, it was only ten years since Honda had launched its first 'real' car, the Civic, and they had not yet produced an engine over 2 litres or a car larger than the Accord. Austin Rover did have a heritage of larger cars and many areas of the company were not prepared to admit that the brilliant concept of Rover SD1 had been seriously flawed in its detailed execution. Almost everything got argued about, with usually some good reason on both sides. One major concession which Honda made very early on was that the new V6 engine, which they would design and supply, would rotate in the conventional direction, unlike all their other engines. As it had to be installed in the same tightly packaged engine compartment as the Austin Rover 4-cylinder power unit which was being developed for the car, this was a very necessary change of strategy for Honda R&D.

The memory of one event during this period has always remained as a graphic illustration of the different corporate cultures at that time. We were having a key meeting at Wako, then the home of Honda R&D, sorting out the plans for the implementation of the project. It had been a series of working meetings with quite large groups from both companies involved and things were generally going quite well, except that our timing people kept insisting that the timing plan was impossible, for Honda as well as for us. When we reconvened after lunch on the last day, I was told that Mr Kume wanted to come and speak to me about something. I expressed pleasure to hear this but quietly wondered what problem had created this visitation.

In came Kume-san and I soon found out! After greetings and introducing him to our team, I said that I understood that he wished to raise something with me. He replied that the relationship between the two companies was now a family affair and in families it was sometimes necessary to speak frankly to one another. With that, he said something in Japanese and two engine trolleys were wheeled in. One contained an O-Series engine which had been taken out of a Princess and looked very much the worse for wear. The other contained a beautifully turned-out prototype Honda 2-litre. He proceeded to lead me around the two, explaining the finer points of engine design and presentation. I was able to reassure him that, although the engine intended for XX was based on the O-Series, it was a very major modification indeed and he need have no concern that the engine compartment of our new joint wonder car would be debased by such an uninspiring looking lump of metal! As the Princess unit was one which had been taken out of a running vehicle which had been standing around outside at Wako for some time, it also demonstrated that comparisons which they made were not always of truly comparable situations. The point was, however, well made; what he was trying to put across was the need for attention to detail and doing the job properly. Ultimately, the M16 engine which was developed from the O-Series turned out to be both a good looker and a good go-er.

We were by now also getting to grips with how the project would be structured, and it had been settled that we would have two Agreements, one to cover the design & development process and related matters, and the other to cover the manufacturing aspects of the project. These documents were highly complex as they were operating manuals as well as legal agreements. The Design & Development Agreement came first and we started work on that during the second half of the year.

Meanwhile, the start of the XX project, and Honda's decision on the direction of rotation for their V6 engine, opened another very welcome opportunity. Austin Rover did not have a transmission to enable the fitting of the 2-litre O-Series engine in LM10/11 (Maestro/Montego). A deal had been done with Volkswagen for them to supply transmissions for the smaller engined versions but these were not suitable for the O-Series. In fact, at that time, no one made a transmission which was compact enough to permit installation in the car, but robust enough to cope with the power and torque of the O-Series 2-litre. Putting it very mildly, this shortage was of major concern to Austin Rover, as the Montego would not be fully competitive without a 2-litre option. Honda's agreement to engineer the transmission, and to lay down the capacity to support Austin Rover's requirements for LM10/11, came as a very considerable relief to a lot of us. When the deal for the supply of the transmission was finalised, the price was also substantially lower than that for the Volkswagen unit. Although it clearly represented useful additional business to Honda, the decision which they took to develop and supply the PG1 for Austin Rover, in the way they did, was a good indication of their willingness to assist their collaborative partner.

Going on in the background at this time were discussions about cars for Australia. In the early 1980s, Australia had quotas for imported vehicles. For historical reasons, Austin Rover Australia had more quota than vehicles it could sell, Honda in Australia had more potential sales than quota. There was thus the basis for a very sensible deal to everyone's advantage and this was done. Honda built and supplied their Quintet model with Rover badges to Austin Rover Australia for sale through their network. As Honda had not sold the Quintet themselves in Australia, it provided the optimum benefit all round.

During this year it became necessary to give serious attention to British Leyland sales in Japan. They were handled at this time by a joint venture company called Leyland Japan. Despite the name, the other partner, Mitsui, was the major shareholder with 60%, British Leyland holding the balance. The company had been established in 1977 and had suffered mightily from shortage of suitable product, the strength of the pound sterling, and the abysmal quality on that product which it did receive. The result was that, by 1982, Mitsui had had enough and wanted out. British Leyland was equally unhappy with the results and initially some discussions were held with Honda to see if they were interested in selling Jaguars in Japan. At that time, Jaguars were the only product with sales potential in Japan; however, one day there would be a Honda-built Rover XX. Honda did have some experience of the import business, as one of their subsidiaries had, in the past, imported and sold American Fords. After due consideration they came back to us and declined our offer, with regret, on the grounds that they needed to concentrate on their volume business in Japan.

As an entertaining aside, one of my Honda colleagues told me at dinner one evening that a contributory factor to their decision had been their experience with the Fords. At that time the main users of large American cars in Japan were the Yakuza, a group of Mafia-like gangsters. The problem was that the quality of the American Fords wasn't very good, which made it difficult to ensure that the customers were kept happy. When the unhappy customers were Yakuza; "it caused a few difficulties". True or not, it was a good story. For a variety of reasons, it was decided that, as I spent so much time and money travelling to Japan, I might as well handle the Leyland Japan takeover in my idle moments.

What started as a fairly straightforward exercise to bring Leyland Japan under full British Leyland ownership suddenly hit a snag. As the only sales of any significance were Jaguars, it had been agreed internally that the new sales company would be owned by Jaguar. This made sense as there was no further product planned for Japan until the launch of the Rover XX, to be built in Japan for the Japanese market, in four years time. The assumption was that the sales company would also sell the XX. This was, of course, before Jaguar's privatisation, which would come in 1984. As there was no fundamental disagreement between British Leyland and Mitsui on the principles, the negotiations were mainly concerned with the financial and commercial arrangements. Cedric Talbot, who became the first President of the new company, and John Turner, who moved from the UK to become the Austin Rover Japan Controller, handled most of this on site as I bounced backwards and forwards between Japan and the UK or, when I was in Japan, between Mitsui and Honda.

Everything seemed to be moving steadily ahead when, late one night in Tokyo, I got a phone call from the UK. It was either Ray Horrocks or Mark Snowdon, I can't remember which. The message was a little disconcerting; Jaguar had decided that they didn't want the pleasure of owning the Japanese company after all. I probably used some totally illegal language over the international telephone link but the key question was - what are we going to do now? We had told Mitsui that we wanted to take over the company and had been negotiating on that basis. To add to the difficulty, we had a meeting with Mitsui the following day at which we were scheduled to sort out the final details for the transfer. The answer to my question did cause some more illegal language, as the gist of it was that nothing had been decided and it was planned to sort it out on my return to the UK. After considering declaring a diplomatic illness and not attending the meeting, we went and told Mitsui that some internal administrative details had come up and we had to sort those out back in the UK. In the end it was agreed that Austin Rover would be the owner of Leyland Japan and would have a contract to be the Jaguar importer/distributor for several years.

During the late summer of 1982 Honda advised us that they now had the plans for the replacement of the Ballade (Acclaim) sorted out internally, were we interested in joining in? As it was less than a year since we had launched the Acclaim there were a few raised eyebrows in Austin Rover, a replacement was certainly not provided for in that time scale in the Corporate Plan. There had to be serious internal discussion, but in the end it was agreed that the opportunity was too good to miss. It was agreed with Honda from the beginning that the project would provide for more Austin Rover identity than had been built into the Acclaim. This was to be provided by the installation of an Austin Rover 1.6-litre engine (being developed for the LM10/11) to supplement the new Honda 1.3-litre engine which was the basic engine for the car. In addition, there would be changes to the front and rear ends to give more of a visual link to other Austin Rover models. The question of identity was of more importance this time, as Honda asked early on if we would build the Ballade version for them to sell in Europe. The project and negotiations got underway quickly, and the decision was made to build the car at Longbridge, as Cowley was submerged in other new product activity (LM10/11 and XX). The 'Acclaim Facelift' as it was codenamed turned into a significant project on two particular counts. Firstly, when launched, it was the first small car carrying the Rover brand since the 'Ten' was discontinued in 1947; secondly, it provided Longbridge with its first Honda experience.

The project did not go as smoothly as its predecessor in terms of the relationship between the companies. Some of this was due to learning from the Acclaim experience, some was due to Honda being difficult, and some was down to Austin Rover. The British Leyland Board had just successfully carried through the great battles with the trade unions which had been so essential. As a result, however, the management style within the company was distinctly abrasive. There were some notable arguments and fallings-out.

1982 continued on its way. At the end of October, Sir Michael Edwardes departed, his place being taken by Sir Austin Bide as non-executive Chairman. Ray Horrocks was head of all the car operations, with David Andrews similarly responsible for commercial vehicles. The whole Japanese front was very busy; the XX project, the Acclaim Facelift, PG1 gearbox supply, the Australian Quintet, and the Leyland Japan takeover were all in active play. Despite the many battles, everything kept moving. The Australian Quintet supply agreement was signed in December. It proved to be a useful bit of business for both companies over several years, but remained outside the mainstream collaboration, being usually handled directly between the Australian company and Honda Export Sales.

Chapter 8
1983: A YEAR OF AGREEMENTS
Anyone else for a nervous breakdown?

The first three months of 1983 were a frenzy of negotiations, with three of the four agreements giving rise to plenty of argument and problems. The PG1 gearbox supply agreement went pretty smoothly, probably because I was only peripherally involved! Only two of the remaining three were with Honda, the third being the takeover of Leyland Japan. By this time, I had managed to explain to Mitsui that we were changing direction and that Austin Rover would be responsible for the company, not Jaguar.

The Acclaim Facelift and XX Design and Development Agreements both gave rise to plenty of argument, both inside the respective companies and between them. On the Acclaim Facelift, the main problems were related to restrictions arising from it being a licensed Honda design. This Agreement was finally signed in May 1983, but without the arrangement for Austin Rover to also build the Honda version being in place. For one reason and another there had been quite a lot of ill-feeling generated over this project, which took some time to overcome.

The XX Agreement had its own problems, though they were somewhat different. The main areas of dispute at this stage were related to the detailed design. What was the right design for a component or system and who should be responsible for executing it? Despite the non-stop wrangling which went on, it kept moving. Just how it kept moving is demonstrated in the final version of the Design and Development Agreement which was signed in late April in Tokyo. The execution copies prepared in London by Freshfields were subjected to further last-minute negotiation and change until late in the evening before the signing, which was scheduled to take place the following morning. Ray Horrocks had arrived that afternoon to sign for British Leyland. I had no option but to stay up for a large portion of the night amending the execution copies by hand. That's how they were signed, and they still exist somewhere in the company archives. That evening there was a very large and jolly celebration dinner when I do remember Mr Kawashima being on very good form. The PG1 Supply Agreement was signed at the same time and so there was good reason for a joint celebration.

The Leyland Japan story still had to be brought to a close, which it was. Armed with what seemed like 20 different powers of attorney, I left for Tokyo yet again to sign the Agreement with Mitsui, pay the 1 Yen price for the company and oversee the establishment of the new Austin Rover Japan. The final meeting with Mitsui created a small problem. The agenda was that, having signed the sale agreements, I would pay the 1 Yen price and receive the Mitsui share certificates. At the last moment I realised that it would not be polite to just chuck a 1 Yen coin across the Mitsui Board Room table, and so Cedric Talbot and I bought a ring box from a jeweller who clearly thought that we were quite mad when we explained that we didn't want a ring, just the box. Particularly when, having got it, we carefully inserted a 1 Yen coin! The box cost us 750 Yen as I recall. It is nice to record that Rover Japan went from strength to strength, becoming a very major force in the Japanese imported car market and a very successful company.

Shortly after this event (which, it must be recorded with regret, did not even merit a message of good wishes from the new owners) we did have an official opening. We were advised that Princess Anne was going to Japan on an official visit and would like to go to a car plant; she would also be happy to help the company if she could. The Princess Royal had been a very loyal and supportive customer for many years. This was splendid news. Firstly, she agreed to carry out an official opening ceremony for Austin Rover Japan which guaranteed excellent publicity; and secondly, we were able to arrange for her to visit the Honda plant at Sayama rather than a competitor's plant and thus kept it all in the family.

The final arrangements were that HRH should have a motor industry day. To Sayama in the morning, then back to Tokyo for her to have lunch with the unbelievably but charmingly named Princess Chichibu, the sister-in-law of Emperor Hirohito. After lunch she would attend an Austin Rover Japan reception in her honour at one of the Tokyo hotels and carry out the official inauguration ceremony. I was invited by Honda to attend at Sayama as the official British Leyland representative, which meant that I would spend the morning and afternoon with the royal party. In the event it was even more involving than I expected. To my surprise the suggestion came from the Embassy that I should go there first thing in the morning, be introduced to the Princess, and then travel as part of the royal party. This was excellent, the only upset being that the timing at the Embassy got a little tight and there was not time to introduce me to HRH. Off we set for Sayama in a cavalcade. This is the only way to defeat the Tokyo traffic, with police motorcycle escorts and the traffic lights ignored all the way. It was bliss to one who seemed to spend too much of life sitting in Tokyo traffic jams!

We arrived at Sayama and the Honda machine went into action, again not leaving enough time for me to be introduced to the Princess which had been the revised plan. Off we all set on the official tour, my friend Shuko Hayashi acting as interpreter for the Princess. I was down the line accompanying HRH's Private Secretary. We had all been equipped with walky-talky radios so that we could hear what was going on at the head of the column. As we set off, I could see that there was a display of vehicles built by the plant (Sayama is Honda's large car plant and at that time built Accords, Preludes and Quintets). Suddenly on the walky-talky we heard the Princess' voice: "what's that?" she demanded in very regal tones. To my utter amazement I heard Shuko reply: "oh, you will have to ask John Bacchus about that." At that moment I didn't even know what 'that' was! HRH must have been utterly confused, not only had she not had her question answered but she was being referred to someone of whom she had never heard for the explanation. 'That' turned out to be an Australian Rover Quintet, which was of course a standard Quintet but with Rover badges. The Princess clearly suspected that her hosts were up to something!

The tour continued uneventfully and at the end we all retired to a conference room for refreshments and for the final formalities. I had still not met the Princess, but now she knew my name. I had earlier been coached about the formality required in conversation with HRH; 'Your Royal Highness' on being introduced, 'Ma'am' thereafter. As we all stood up to leave, the Princess had to walk past me on her way out. To my amazement, as she reached me, she paused and said: "will you be at the reception this afternoon?" "Yes Ma'am" I stammered, realising as I said it that it should have been 'Your Royal Highness'. "Right," she said, "see you there." So much for the protocol! The reception went very well and the Princess gave us more time than her programme provided, giving the company an excellent send-off. I did explain about the Quintet in the afternoon. Getting back to the XX Manufacturing Agreement negotiations seemed rather a letdown after that.

One development during 1983 was not widely publicised but was actually of some significance. This was the Agreement in Principle that we should build the PG1 transmission rather than import it fully built from Japan. We had gone to Tokyo for one of our one-day flying visits which were a speciality of Harold Musgrove (Chairman of Austin Rover Group). This one was for a Sunday meeting with Mr Kume. The meeting was held at the Palace Hotel to discuss some issues which had arisen on the XX project. During the course of the discussions, we suggested that we should build the V6 engine in the UK. It was not a surprise when Mr Kume politely, firmly, and without delay declined the offer. What followed was unexpected, however. Harold Musgrove accepted Mr Kume's position on the engine without further argument, but countered with a demand to build the PG1 transmission instead. This was a surprise to everyone as we had only just signed the Agreement for the supply of the built-up transmission, and Austin Rover had been following a quite specific policy of not investing in transmission design and manufacture. The Agreement provided for Austin Rover to negotiate terms for a manufacturing licence after a period of supply, however none of us had envisaged kicking this into play so quickly. Very much to my surprise, after some discussion with his colleagues, Mr Kume agreed in principle and we set in motion what was to be the longest active Agreement between the companies. It was an Agreement which turned out to be surprisingly difficult to finalise and one which caused disagreement between the parties at various stages during its negotiation.

During this time there was a fairly steady level of activity on the V6 engine front. It was at this stage that Honda informed us that the original 3-valve concept wasn't giving the target results and would have to be changed to a 4-valve. This had two results; the price increased fairly substantially; and the dimensions of the engine also increased. The price increase had to be sorted and fought over, but initially we did not think that the increase in size would cause a major problem. When they gave us the news, Honda said that they had checked the under-bonnet situation and the only problem created by the new engine was that the bonnet profiles would have to be modified slightly.

This should not have been a significant concern, as we had previously agreed that no tooling commitment would be made by either party without prior advice to the other. Unfortunately, there had been a hole in the Austin Rover toolroom programme and, rather than paying people for doing nothing, a decision had been taken to start the Rover 800 (XX) bonnet tooling. For some reason this message had not been given to anyone to pass on to Honda. Under all normal circumstances, the decision would have been quite correct and reasonable; however this was a joint project and Honda were very reluctant to admit to problems until they also had the solution. The result was that we had the bonnet tooling well advanced by the time we received the message. As so often under these circumstances, there were faults on both sides. It did lead to major argument between the companies before it was sorted out, with a financial contribution from Honda towards the cost of the redundant tooling.

As well as the commercial issues on the V6 engine there was also a fairly constant technical debate on the performance characteristics of the engine. As launched, it was 2.5-litres in displacement and, although very powerful for its time, needed high revs. This is a feature of Honda engines generally but did cause concern within Austin Rover, and there were several meetings when the subject was debated fairly acrimoniously. Honda R&D did not welcome any criticism of their work, particularly on engines. They clearly did recognise the deficiency, as the 2.7-litre was put in hand very early on. As usual there was no acknowledgment of a problem until the solution was clearly identified and underway.

1983 continued with ongoing argument and negotiation on everything, but mainly around the XX, both the project itself and the 'Manufacturing Agreement'. This Agreement was very complex, as it defined the operating principles under which the vehicles would be built, and how we would sell them to one another. Since we were making up the rules as we went along, it was extremely stimulating and challenging, as well as providing plenty of opportunity for disagreement. Into this already complex and contentious arena now came the serious consideration of the method of Austin Rover's re-entry into the US market.

This intention had been made clear to, and accepted by Honda, from the early days of the XX project. Now we started to talk in detail about the method and the problems began. Honda had assumed that we would re-enter through the existing, old-established subsidiary then located in Leonia, New Jersey and selling only Jaguars. The Austin Rover sports car range had been run out by 1981 and the Rover SD1 had been withdrawn even earlier. Jaguar had by this time taken over Leonia internally in preparation for privatisation. What ensued illustrated well the difference in attitude between a British and Japanese company.

Although the pending privatisation of Jaguar (which would take place in July 1984) was an open secret it was not discussed in any detail with Honda. To them, privatised or unprivatised, it was unthinkable that the Rover 800 should be sold into the USA through any route other than the company which became Jaguar Inc. As far as the Jaguar and Austin Rover managements were concerned that was the very last thing to be contemplated. This unusual degree of agreement between the two British Leyland groups was utterly incomprehensible to the Japanese and so, when Austin Rover started to talk about trying to do a deal with one of the US majors for them to import and distribute the car, Honda was not amused at the thought of contributing to a project which might significantly benefit one of its major competitors in the US market. This situation kept bubbling but finally came to a head at the last minute, before the signing of the XX Manufacturing Agreement in April 1984. The final negotiations carried on until literally the last moment in the Portman Hotel in Portman Square, London, with the signatories waiting in the wings. In the end it was settled with a compromise, and eventually an ill-fated deal with Braman Enterprises in Florida was set up to handle sales of the Rover Sterling in the USA. But that is another story.

1983 saw a major and unexpected change in the relationship. This was the retirement of Mr Kawashima as President of Honda and his replacement by Mr Kume. It all seemed very strange to us, as we had become so used to the 'upheaval' style of management change which was, and remained for many years, a feature of British Leyland. Mr Kawashima was a very active, relatively young man, and the company had certainly prospered under his leadership. He told us that it was time to hand over to a younger man and, in October 1983, that is what he did. This change also established the principle that the Presidential seat was always occupied by an R&D man, regardless of the existence of more senior Executive Vice-Presidents. Mr Kume was in fact a Senior Managing Director immediately prior to being appointed President.

An early styling model of the British Leyland version of XX, which would become the Rover 800, dated 18 June 1982. It has been signed off by Gordon Sked (stylist) and Roy Axe (head of the Austin Rover Design Studio)

Design sketches for the Honda version of XX, the Legend, dated 31 July 1982.

This is a styling model for the Honda Legend, probably in the studio at the Honda R&D facility, Wako, in Japan. Styling sketches are visible on the wall behind. The picture is dated 28 September 1982.

While XX was still in progress, the two companies embarked on another project for a smaller car. Known internally as the 'Acclaim Facelift' this car would become the Rover 200 and second generation Honda Ballade.

This clay model is for the Honda version of the Acclaim Facelift, pictured at Wako on 2 June 1983.

The British Leyland version of the Acclaim Facelift on view at Longbridge in 1983. Note the badge on the front grille, showing that the decision to give it a Rover identity has been made.

The Rover 200 production line at Longbridge in 1984. This Vanden Plas version has reached the rolling road at the end of the assembly hall where it is being tested for the performance of brakes, acceleration and gears.

The Rover 200 had a more varied model range than the Triumph Acclaim. This 216 Vitesse had the larger Rover 1.6 litre engine and a sporty body style and interior.

1984, the Rover 200 in CAB2 at Longbridge. Another version of 'stuff-up', though this time for the rear suspension components of the car.

Chapter 9
1984: GATHERING MOMENTUM
Austin Rover Swindon gets a neighbour

One of the milestones that was passed at this time was the decision to badge the Acclaim Facelift as the Rover 200. It should be mentioned in this context that the concept of what later became known as 'Roverisation' was already being developed. Mark Snowdon was emphatic that the car should be badged as a Rover and after much internal discussion he convinced the rest of the company. The hope was that the Rover marque would move the company upmarket, and help to shed the reputation for unreliability and poor quality which had become associated with its other brands. Opinions were divided on the subject, I had my own reservations, not about the principle, but whether the car, which was really a Civic 4-door, was up to the job. The decision was the right one and the car helped to lay the foundations for what was to follow.

The preparations for production continued at Longbridge, but it became quite clear that the Honda-engined versions would have to be launched first, before the 1.6-litre version, which eventually followed some six months later. The project did not go as smoothly as the Acclaim. It was more complex, with more change from the original Honda design, including the installation of a power unit which was completely different to that for which the car had been designed. Mr Nobuhiko Kawamoto, who was at this time President of Honda R&D, was always very unhappy about the engine change, and Mr Kume had to do a lot of convincing to get him to agree. It all worked reasonably well in the end, although the 1.6-litre car did not have the trouble-free performance of the 1.3-litre. We had a lot to learn, and there was still a lot of resistance to the learning. At this time there remained a fundamental belief that the quality and reliability problems would be solved with the next new model.

In the immediate aftermath of the signing of the XX Manufacturing Agreement in April, we launched into a round of strategic discussions about the future development of the relationship. Honda presented us with their proposals, which we found to be quite challenging. In summary they proposed to develop their position in Europe, with Austin Rover as an integral part of their strategy. Their basic plan involved the establishment, by them, of a local manufacturing plant which would build both engines and vehicles, together with the setting up of a joint programme similar to XX for a smaller European car. The key elements were that Austin Rover would build both versions of the car for Europe, using engines supplied from the proposed Honda plant. Honda would build both versions of the car in Japan, as with XX. As a lead-in to this situation they also requested that we build the Ballade version of the Acclaim Facelift for them to sell in Europe. As can be imagined this caused some very serious thought and discussion for British Leyland, where the future was a little uncertain.

The position was unsettled, the euphoria of the Metro launch was long gone, the Maestro had been launched to a not overwhelmingly enthusiastic public, despite getting a lot of publicity for being the first British-designed talking car. At the same time, the question of exhaust emission legislation began to be seriously pushed by the European Commission; Austin Rover knew that meeting the type of standards being proposed would be a major, and expensive task for the generally ageing engine range. This message was of course relayed to Her Majesty's Government, who were then in the pincers. They were negotiating their position with the European Commission and the other member governments; at the same time 'their' car company was telling them that it would create a need for even more cash than had been provided for in the Corporate Plans. They did not find this very amusing and so, when it was combined with a situation whereby the new in-house products were not meeting their financial, volume or quality objectives, it was hardly surprising that we were not the Prime Minister's favourite motor company. This was not helped by the situation in the Department for Trade and Industry, where a succession of Secretaries of State passed by so quickly that if you blinked there was a risk of missing one.

The engine question was particularly sensitive. Austin Rover was working on the concept which became the K-Series engine. The need for this was reinforced by the impending exhaust emission legislation, where there was serious concern that the venerable A-series engine might not be capable of meeting the standards efficiently. With the K-Series not yet an approved programme, and a far from enthusiastic shareholder, the idea of a Honda engine plant somewhere in the UK was cause for concern. The idea of a Maestro replacement at the right time, and in collaboration with Honda, was more appealing, particularly with the potential of the supply of substantial volume to Honda. It was also quite clear that the Government viewed the development of the relationship with some favour.

There was a lot of discussion that summer, most of it in the UK, as the Honda people were also sorting out where their plant should be. It was agreed that we would set a target to have a sound Statement of Understanding, which would define the way ahead, signed by the end of the year. Austin Rover was in a very nervous state at this time. There was a serious concern that Honda's plan to build a vehicle plant was a signal that they were preparing to walk away from us, or that, at the very least, they would use its existence as a lever to negotiate unacceptable terms for vehicle build from Austin Rover. One thing we knew for certain was that the Government would not do anything to discourage Honda from building a plant. Opinions in the company were, as ever, divided. Some saw it all as a fiendish plot to damage Austin Rover, some were concerned that it would provide the Government with a stick to beat Austin Rover with, and some felt that the whole thing could be made to work to the benefit of both.

We did move ahead and, by late summer, the vehicle concept was beginning to firm up. We were hitting a problem, however, which was introduction timing. Austin Rover had launched the Maestro in 1983 and the Rover 200 in July 1984; the new car would replace both, but the Corporate Plan had assumed a model life of at least six years for each of them. Honda wanted to see a vehicle launch before then, but we were already telling the Government that we needed more capital expenditure because of the emissions programme. The timing proposed by Honda would increase the requirement for capital expenditure within the plan period. Nevertheless, as we approached the end of the year, the draft Statement of Understanding was beginning to take shape. Honda had decided upon Swindon for its plant, which would commence operations as an inspection centre for imported vehicles, XXs and (probably) Ballades built by Austin Rover for Honda.

During 1984 we had also launched the Montego, and running through the year there had been ongoing negotiations on the PG1 transmission licence agreement, which was proving to be quite difficult to deliver. The supply of built-up gearboxes from Japan was going ahead very well, with a minor problem on gear noise which was sorted eventually. Honda had no incentive to do a deal which took money out of their pockets, Austin Rover also had some demands to which they took exception, and eventually we came to an impasse. I then had to tell the Austin Rover Board that they couldn't have the deal on the terms on which they insisted. Harold Musgrove was not one to react happily to not getting his own way, but there was no alternative on this one. In the end we gave a bit and they gave a bit, some words were changed and the deal was done. For many years it performed well as a gearbox; but still, from time to time it caused problems between the companies on either component costs from Honda, or British Leyland's wish to re-source components away from Honda supply. The real villain was, of course, the increasing strength of the Yen against the pound sterling as the years went by.

Everything seemed to be moving in the right direction, but against a background of considerable uncertainty around the Corporate Plan funding. The combination of the need for substantial expenditure for the European emission requirements, with a failure to deliver the volume performance previously projected, was causing the Government to press for a stringent review of the Capital Expenditure Plan. Inevitably, progress on the Statement of Understanding slowed down as a result of this and so we were not able to finalise and sign it by the end of the year as planned. Honda were by this time used to the annual Corporate Plan review with the Department of Trade And Industry but as, in the past, this had always been resolved without causing them any significant problems, they did not get too concerned at the delay.

In 1987 the M16 engine won a British Design Award. This picture shows the head of Power Train, Roland Bertodo (front centre right) with his development/design team.

The K-series engine project began in 1984 and was badly needed in the face of Austin Rover's rapidly ageing engine range in an era of ever changing emission regulations. It first went into service as a 1.4-litre power unit in the Rover 200 (R8) of 1989. Over the years many versions, in different capacities, would be developed. On the right is the KV6 which was introduced with the 1996 Rover 800 facelift.

Chapter 10
1985: FOCUS ON ENGINES
A year of engines and interesting discussions

The beginning of the year saw the finalisation and signing of the PG1 transmission licence Agreement. We continued to develop the Statement of Understanding and the vehicle concept which was at its core. An agreed draft was completed by late March, but it then ran into difficulties, as the Corporate Plan remained unapproved by the Department of Trade and Industry and so we could not sign the Statement of Understanding. This now started to be a problem with Honda, even though they had become used to the cliff-hanging of previous years, right back to the original Acclaim Agreement signing. This delay was much longer than previously experienced and the settlement of the strategy set out in the Statement of Understanding was crucial to Honda's own European strategy. They wanted to get moving and did start to express concern. The Government was very aware of this aspect and was very keen to ensure that Honda should not be turned off, as they were now talking seriously about their UK manufacturing operation. Messages of the 'don't worry' type from the Department of Trade and Industry were transmitted by me to Honda, which kept things simmering; however, it was June before we were able to sign the document. Fortunately, we had both pressed on with the vehicle project and so there was little real damage done.

At about this time some light relief was provided by Kiyoshi Ikemi's triumphant victory in a long-running, friendly needle match. Kiyoshi had gone to university in the USA and spoke fluent American-English. As mentioned elsewhere he always did the translating at our top management meetings. Following one particular incident at a meeting in the UK, when Harold Musgrove misunderstood Kiyoshi's use of the Americanism "if you guys will buy that", thinking it meant 'purchase' rather than the intended 'agree with', I used to tease Kiyoshi that he translated from Japanese to American and I then translated from American to English for the benefit of our people. He would usually rise to this one.

Not very long after Honda had moved into their new headquarters building in Aoyama in Tokyo, I arrived for a visit. I knew that Prince Charles and Princess Diana had visited Honda a few days earlier during their visit to Japan and expected to hear something about the visit, probably when initial business had been dealt with. Not so; the gleeful greeting which I received was: "I've finally got you fixed." It transpired that he had acted as the interpreter for the royal couple's visit to Honda and, as they were leaving, Prince Charles had turned to Kiyoshi, thanked him for his help, and said: "Mr Ikemi, I must commend you on your ENGLISH." Mr Ikemi then insisted that, as my future King thought his English was so good, who was I to make jokes about it? I capitulated.

Behind all this was a great deal of activity on the development of Austin Rover's engine plans. European emission requirements were putting a major emphasis on the need for significant action and expenditure. The K-Series and the in-house Zeta V6 engine projects were both now being seriously investigated and were moving towards requiring approval. The K-Series was of primary importance and, as a high-volume engine programme, required a large capital investment. The engine was urgently required, both for the new joint car with Honda, and for the intended Metro replacement, the AR6. The A-series had done valiant service since it was introduced for the Austin A30 in 1951 in 803 cc form, but everyone was agreed that we could not contemplate putting it into these new cars. It was not refined enough for sophisticated cars of the planned new breed and, in any case, there were serious doubts being expressed about its ability to meet the emission standards.

There was great determination in Austin Rover to see the K-series project through, but it did require a very substantial investment and the majority shareholder - the British Government - was insisting that capital expenditure be cut back. Somebody (in Whitehall) then had a bright idea; Honda and British Leyland work together! Honda were planning to manufacture engines in their proposed UK plant to supply Austin Rover with some of their requirements for the new joint car. The logical thing was to get Honda to invest the additional money to provide the capacity to meet all Austin Rover's engine requirements. It was, however, important to maintain the position that the Government did not interfere in the running of the business, and so a British Leyland team of Harold Musgrove and Mike Carver, supported by myself and Ron MacIntosh (then Austin Rover's chief power train engineer) were despatched to ask Honda if they were prepared to do this. This mission was a somewhat difficult one. We had spent the past several months insisting to Honda that the new car must accommodate the K-series engine and that we would only use engines from the Honda UK plant in jointly developed cars. At the time of this meeting the Statement of Understanding was also not yet signed, so there was still a question mark over the future for both companies.

The result of the meeting was that Mr Kume stated that Honda was not in a position to accede to this request. This decision must have been made with some difficulty, as Honda did not want to offend the British Government, but at the same time certainly did not want to be seen to be taking a substantial amount of work away from Austin Rover. In the event, when the message was fed back to the British Leyland Board and the Department of Trade and Industry, the Corporate Plan was approved and the K-series went ahead. It seems quite simple now but at the time it was all pretty tense. The whole episode was, I'm sure, duly noted in the corridors of power.

There was plenty to get on with. The XX project was getting closer to delivery and the new project, codenamed R8/YY, was now beginning to move. This somewhat clumsy designation was a good example of how pragmatic we all became. In informal discussions the label YY had been used; however, when we came to formalise the situation, it was pointed out that our 'friends' in the UK media would welcome the opportunity to have 'Why? Why?' headlines, when they became aware of the project. Honda were already used to simple codenames with 'XX' and so, to keep everyone comfortable, R8/YY it became.

The XX project was creating its own problems. Technical and commercial difficulties were being solved by the deceptively simple solution of sacrificing commonality between the two versions. By the time that a halt was called to this process, the damage had been done and the seeds of the US Rover 800 Sterling disaster were well and truly sown, together with many quality problems which would cause trouble on the Rover 800 in other markets.

The Honda version of XX, the Legend, was now rolling towards its launch in Japan in the autumn. We were in some difficulties with the Rover 800, and by this time it was clear that our earliest launch timing would be summer 1986, and that would be with the Honda V6 engine only. The version with an Austin Rover 2-litre engine, the major volume seller, would have to follow later. This was a big disappointment but with it did come, in some Austin Rover people, an acceptance that it wasn't all Honda's fault and that, just maybe, there were things which we could, and should learn from them.

We were also getting on with defining the framework and timing of the R8/YY project. The overall approach was to be similar to XX, but we both agreed that it was absolutely essential to learn from the mistakes of XX. This quickly translated itself into a proposal which Mr Kawamoto made to me that: "we'll design it and you build it." In practice it was far more complex than that, but did avoid the problems of XX which had been created by the shared-out design responsibility. As with XX, the complication of accommodating the Honda and Rover engines had to be taken care of. Although they were both, in this case, 4-cylinder units, there was the additional complexity created by them rotating in opposite directions.

The concept, hard points, and timing were agreed and we were off with a 5-door hatchback, which would be the right size for us to replace both Maestro and Rover 200, to be launched in 1989. The styling and preliminary engineering work commenced in Japan with a resident Austin Rover team, led by Mike Pendry, in place. This time it worked, and a basically common style with clear identity differences was agreed to the satisfaction of both companies.

There were wide ranging discussions on other matters arising from the Statement of Understanding. One which did have a direct result was the decision that Austin Rover would, after all, build Honda Ballade versions of the Rover 200, which was then in production at Longbridge, as a practice run for building the Honda version of R8/YY. As this would only have a limited life, it was agreed that it would be in right-hand-drive form only for the UK. It was also agreed that Honda would supply our Australian company with a Rover badged version of their Integra model which was a more luxurious and stylish replacement for the Quintet.

The discussions leading up to the Statement of Understanding had also included the consideration of a possible British Leyland shareholding in the Honda UK plant. This did not get into very serious discussion at the time, as there wasn't any money to spare for that, and anyway it would have meant, in effect, that the British Government would have been investing in the Honda plant. The question of shareholdings remained the subject of recurring discussion until the cross-shareholding deal was finally done in 1990. We were also pressing Honda to let us build unique vehicles for them at Cowley, thus seeking to avoid the installation of additional capacity at Honda Swindon. In the end the whole issue of the build of unique Honda vehicles was put on the back burner and we got on with the joint projects; including, of course, the development of the Honda Swindon plant as an engine producer for R8/YY, as well as a vehicle inspection and rectification centre for both imported cars and those produced by Austin Rover for Honda.

In the background other things were going on, particularly on the engine scene. At this time, Austin Rover had five new engines under development:

- K-SERIES: 1.1 and 1.4-litre versions
- L16 SERIES: 1.6-litre 4-valve head version of S-series (not to be confused with the 1995 L-Series turbo-diesel)
- M16: 2-litre 4-valve for the Rover 800
- MDi: 2-litre direct injection diesel, a joint project with Perkins
- ZETA: V6 engine, the design and development of which was to be sub-contracted to Porsche.

Since we couldn't possibly afford all of these, collaborative projects were seen as very desirable.

To progress this, contact was established with Ford of Europe; Mark Snowdon and I met a small Ford team in London. To my great pleasure they were led by my last boss at Ford, Ron Mellor, who had now become Vice-President, Engineering. We had always had a very good relationship and I felt sure that if there was any possibility of collaboration, Ron and I would find a way to achieve it. After a couple of meetings, it was clear that they were interested in the K-Series, and we started preparing some engineering information to give to them. Then, one morning, Ron rang me with the surprise message to put a stop on us sending them any information. He was quite upset but told me that, despite the genuine interest by Ford of Europe, they had been told to 'back off' by 'Corporate' (in other words Ford's US Headquarters at Dearborn, Michigan). We agreed to freeze everything for the time being, because he hoped to get it moving again inside Ford.

We were both in total ignorance of the real reason for this apparently unjustified objection from Dearborn. What we didn't know was that Ford had approached the Government proposing to buy Austin Rover. This had coincided with a similar approach from General Motors for Land Rover. It was all kept very confidential, with a small team in each company in the know, and no-one else. At this stage I was not informed of the development and so felt very irritated with Ford HQ.

There was a bit of light relief in 1985 (at my expense). Our Public Affairs Director at this time was Jean Denton (later Baroness Denton). She decided that she wanted to present a different image for the company and persuaded Harold Musgrove that I should be interviewed by the *Financial Times*, talking about the Honda relationship. The timing would also enable us to take a positive position on the Legend launch in Japan, and set the scene for the Rover 800 launch in 1986.

It was all set up and I spent a couple of hours talking with Kenneth Gooding, the journalist concerned. It all seemed to go well, despite my innate mistrust of the 'Fourth Estate' and I was left feeling that the resulting article would be constructive. Then it appeared. As an article it was good publicity for the company, a positive half page in the *Financial Times* has to be of value, but the personal cost was terrible. In the opening section of the article I was described thus: 'John Bacchus, a cheerful, chubby individual of 48'. I still carry the psychological scars of the comments I received from family, colleagues and alleged friends as a result of the publication of those words. Even Harold took to addressing me as 'Fatty'. Journalists - huh!

The result of the XX project, Rover 800, would go into production at Cowley in 1986.

By the mid 1980s there was a major drive to improve the quality and reliability of the company's products. As part of this, new techniques were introduced into the production process. Here, an under bonnet assurance check is being carried out on a Rover 800, using a new 'talking computer' system.

These 'men in white coats' are undertaking checks during a quality audit on one of the Rover 800 bodyshells from the Cowley production line.

The other side of the quality drive was information and training for both managers and production line workers. This booklet, *Tomorrow, Today*, accompanied a film shown in training sessions.

The cutaway diagram shows the impressive engineering of the Rover 800. Fitting the various sizes of power unit into the compact engine bay had been challenging.

It was a major coup when, in July 1986, Margaret Thatcher agreed to participate in a photoshoot outside Downing Street with the just-launched Rover 800. Harold Musgrove was on hand to explain the finer details. Everything was going well, as the normally sceptical Prime Minister praised the car, until she unhelpfully added: "if only I could afford one."

Government papers released in 2017 revealed that Rover were careful to avoid the blunder made a few years earlier when they supplied a red Maestro for a similar event. This time, they made sure the car was a distinguished 'Tory' blue.

Graham Day was Chairman of Rover Group from 1986-91 and oversaw the sale to British Aerospace

George Simpson was recruited by Graham Day as Managing Director of Rover Group and succeeded him as Chairman (1991-94)

Tadashi Kume, Head of R&D in the early 1980s, succeeded Kiyoshi Kawashima as Honda President (1983-90)

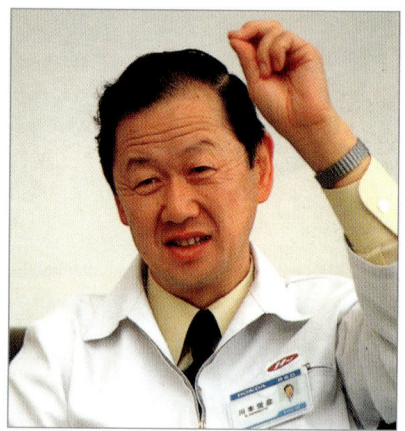
Nobuhiko Kawamoto was also Head of R&D before succeeding Tadashi Kume as Honda President (1990-98)

Les Wharton, Managing Director Rover Group

Tony Rose, Finance Director Rover Group

John Towers, Managing Director Rover Group

Chapter 11
1986: THINGS GET HECTIC!
Enter the F-word: Ford makes a bid; followed by a few changes

My passport tells me that, by the end of January, not only had I visited Tokyo twice, I had also fitted in a visit to India. I may have been jet-lagged! We were active in India at this time, and Mark Snowdon had agreed to deliver the keynote speech at the 25th anniversary gathering of the Indian equivalent of the Society of Motor Manufacturers and Traders. This was due to take place in conjunction with the Delhi Motor Show, early in the New Year. During the Christmas holiday, I had a phone call from Mark. He apologised that he couldn't tell me much at the moment, but something had come up which prevented him going to India. Would I please take his place? This was no great problem, except that his speech had already been sent ahead for publication, and so I would have to deliver it as he had written it. His approach to a speech was very different to mine, but it got presented. This was an entertaining start to the year. My real problem was not knowing what was going on. I was desperate to know what could cause Mark to change his plans for an important public appearance at such short notice.

On my return to the UK from India, I was quickly admitted to membership of the very limited group who were party to the 'Maverick' project. Ford had approached the Government proposing to buy Austin Rover Group Ltd (which was a subsidiary of British Leyland Ltd, the company in which the Government held shares). This had followed on from an unsuccessful attempt on their part to arrange a merger of some form between Ford of Europe and Fiat. One can only speculate at what the initial reaction to this approach must have been in Downing Street. It must have seemed, just before Christmas, that Santa had come early and his name was Henry. The British Leyland Board was not so sure, seeing itself as having responsibilities to the workforce as well as to the shareholder. The majority of the Austin Rover Board was quite sure – no way! They were quite clear that it would mean the closure of at least one of the main plants, probably Cowley, and total absorption into badge-engineered Ford product. Another question was, what about Honda? They clearly had to be told, and quickly, and their reaction sought. By this time the Whitehall position was quite cautious, the possible effects on employment were being recognised and they also saw the Honda implications.

In mid-January a team led by Ray Horrocks went to Tokyo. The group also included a senior official from the Department of Trade and Industry to formally advise Honda of what was happening and of the British Government's position. It was important to bring Honda into the picture for several reasons:

- It was only six months since the companies had signed the Statement of Understanding, with the Government's full support.

- The existing contracts between the companies provided the option for their speedy termination if either were to be taken over by another car company.
- What about XX (in mid-launch) and R8/YY (just getting under way)?
- The British Government would prefer not to upset Honda, which had supported British Leyland and was building its own new plant in the UK.
- Ford had already asked Honda for a private meeting.

The outcome of the meeting between Honda, British Leyland and the Department of Trade and Industry, was that Mr Kume received the underlying message and clearly understood that, whilst British Leyland was opposed to the proposal, the British Government's position was not as negative. Certainly, their declared policy was to get all of British Leyland privatised and the process was already underway.

At this stage Honda expressed the wish to avoid involvement; however they did confirm that, if the takeover went ahead, then they would definitely reconsider the nature of their relationship with Austin Rover. They did not have any intention of entering into a relationship with Ford of the type they had with us. They would meet with Ford but only to hear what they had to say. It was clearly a very difficult position for them, trying to balance their interests and relationships with Austin Rover and the British Government whilst being, at the same time, determined not to be swept into a relationship with Ford. Our understanding was that Ford was very keen to inherit the relationship and anxious to reassure Honda that they would be welcome members of the family. There had been serious discussions between Honda and Ford in the early 1970's.

I stayed on in Tokyo to get direct feedback from the meeting between Ford and Honda, and also to attempt to get an informal understanding of how Honda really felt about the situation. It was all quite undramatic really. According to Honda, the meeting with Ford went smoothly and politely, with Honda maintaining their position. In the private discussions which we had subsequently, they did assure me that, if it did happen, they would not take any precipitate action on existing contracts. The R8/YY as a joint project, however, would be stopped.

The position Honda took on the existing contracts was not all that popular in Austin Rover, where a statement from Honda that they would terminate all arrangements forthwith, if the takeover occurred, would have been welcomed as useful ammunition in the battle. Honda were being very careful to ensure that they would be seen to do the right thing if it did happen. They had their own future and interests to consider. Quite simply, they did not want to see Austin Rover sold to Ford as it would interfere with their strategy for Europe; at the same time they recognised that the British Government was keen to see privatisation and they did not want to upset them. They took a very mature and sensible approach to a difficult situation. As a measure of this, despite their position regarding R8/YY, work continued unabated.

One thing which did come out of these informal discussions was a confirmation that, if the Ford bid failed and privatisation proceeded via a consortium of institutional investors, as was the expected route, then Honda might be prepared to consider the possibility of joining such a consortium. At this early stage they established the position that they wished to see Austin Rover remain as a British company, a position they maintained right up to the BMW purchase of Rover Group in 1994.

The Ford/British Leyland meetings continued, I was not directly involved and did not take part in any of the face-to-face meetings with Ford. My task was to be kept up to date with developments and to keep Honda informed to the extent necessary. It was also important to ensure that Honda had a secure communication channel to us. It was a strange period, because only a very small number of people knew about the Ford approach, and so one existed on two different planes for about two months. Ford was basically trying to carry out a due diligence investigation with an unwilling supplier of information. There were always heated denials, but many of us felt that the Department of Trade and Industry pushed Austin Rover to provide information to Ford which subsequently was of significant commercial benefit to them. The discussions continued and so did everything else. We had to carry on as though nothing was happening in order to ensure that security was maintained.

Work continued on the R8/YY project and Mike Pendry and his engineering team were very busy in their long assignment in Japan. They were working very hard at Wako on the styling and feasibility engineering, in conjunction with Honda R&D, and were living at the Century Hyatt in Shinjuku. There was quite a crowd of them and I have deeply embedded memories of going into the Tradewinds Bar in the hotel for a nightcap and finding 'the Pendry bunch' well established. There was an instant and pressing invitation to join them, with no prizes for guessing who finished up with the bar bill on these occasions! We were also fighting our way through the Agreement covering the manufacture of the Honda Ballade (the Honda version of the first Rover 200) to supply to them. The Rover 200 had been launched in 1984 and, although we had originally backed away from manufacturing the Ballade for Honda, it had now been agreed in principle as part of the R8/YY package. We got the Agreement sorted out and signed in April 1986.

Behind all this, the real excitement was happening. In late February or early March, the news leaked simultaneously of General Motors' bid for Land Rover and Ford's bid for Austin Rover. The Government was still suffering from the after-effects of the Westland Helicopters affair, which had caused an embarrassing public row about whether or not Britain's last surviving helicopter manufacturer should be rescued by a European consortium or sold to an American company. This resulted in yet another change of Secretary of State at the Department of Trade and Industry and much heated press coverage. The prospect of these foreign takeovers of two parts of British Leyland made for good, media-induced, jingoistic hysteria, particularly regarding Land Rover, which was quickly picked up in the Palace of Westminster. The Government decided that enough was enough, and fairly quickly a statement was made ending both sets of talks. This was hailed as a great success in Austin Rover and life quickly returned to what passed for normal. There was one postscript. Quite soon after the formal end of discussions, I rang Ron Mellor to say that we were interested in picking up the earlier discussions on engine collaboration which had been put on hold. Ron's immediate response was enthusiastic agreement, but it had to be checked with 'Corporate'. In the end he called me to say that it had been decided, as a matter of policy, not to proceed.

At about this time, the announcement was made that British Leyland was to have a new Chairman. Sir Austin Bide, who had been non-executive Chairman since the departure of Michael Edwardes in 1982, was to retire. He would be replaced as an Executive Chairman by Graham Day, a Canadian who had been the boss of British Shipbuilders. The assumption followed that this would lead to some management restructuring. In due course this proved to be very much the case. Graham made his presence felt from the start. Two early casualties were Ray Horrocks and David Andrews, who both resigned shortly after his appointment.

This co-incided with the decision to rename British Leyland Ltd as Rover Group Plc, a move which it was hoped would improve the Corporation's tarnished image. One thing which came through very quickly was that he saw the Honda relationship as being of fundamental importance to the future of the car operations. At one of our earliest meetings at the new Corporate Headquarters in Hobart Place, London, Mike Carver, Mark Snowdon and I were having a strategy discussion with Graham. Mark made some statement boosting Austin Rover; I cannot remember what the subject was, but I do remember Graham retorting that he had examined it very closely and: "the only thing worth a goddam is the Honda relationship." This attack was rather hard on Mark who had been a very active and important protagonist of the relationship from the beginning.

The problems were building up on the Rover 800. The Honda Legend had already started production in Japan in October 1985. It was launched straight away in Japan, followed by the USA in the spring of 1986. Reaction in Japan had been disappointing for Honda, but the Americans were taking to their first Japanese luxury car with great enthusiasm. By contrast, it had become quite clear that the planned UK launch date of early spring 1986 for the Rover 800 was unachievable, because the new Rover M16 engine was not yet ready. Harold Musgrove was having to accept that, despite his greatest efforts and his passionate belief in Austin Rover, the parts of the programme for which we were responsible were the areas causing problems.

The launch programme for the summer did go ahead, but only with the Honda V6-engined versions, meaning that all the emphasis was placed on the top end of the range. This was a mistake from which we were to suffer in the UK market, as it resulted in the car acquiring a reputation for being expensive. This was bolstered by the particularly unfortunate backfiring of a part of the launch publicity. It had been arranged for Harold Musgrove to be at Number Ten Downing Street, with a car to demonstrate to Mrs Thatcher for the benefit of the television cameras. This all went well, the Prime Minister was shown the car, drove it, climbed out, looked straight at the cameras and said that it was a very impressive car; and then she added that she wished she could afford one. The message was given and, for a long time, the public perception of the range was that it was very expensive; after all the Prime Minister, who was always seen being driven in her Jaguar, had said so. It was a most unfortunate gaffe, and undoubtedly combined with the launch strategy to establish an overly high-priced image which, I am sure, lost us sales in the first year or two.

The Ford affair had concentrated everyone's minds and that, combined with the arrival of Graham Day, created an environment conducive to serious discussion about the future form of the Honda relationship. These talks were at the top Rover Group level, rather than subsidiary Austin Rover Group level. I did, however, remain fully involved, despite my official position being within Austin Rover. We were all sure that Graham's brief was to promote the move towards privatisation as soon as possible. In this context Austin Rover was a problem, as it had no consistent profit record, just the reverse. A really firm relationship with Honda which had a highly successful public image, would be a definite attraction to the type of institutional investors who would be looked to as members of a consortium for privatisation. So, as well as the routine operational aspects of XX and R8/YY (which were anything but routine), we were talking to Honda about many complex organisational issues.

First, was the possibility of them taking a shareholding in a privatised Austin Rover. Honda was lukewarm on the shareholding question at this stage. As the plans for privatisation by consortium were theoretical, it was difficult to move much further other than agreeing that, if and when it became a reality, they would consider it. On one aspect they were quite positive, and that was that they would only consider taking a small shareholding of less than 20%. They would not consider any level of holding which would imply management responsibility or a public image of control.

Second, was the suggestion that Austin Rover should build Honda vehicles which were not part of collaborative projects, in order to avoid Honda themselves building cars at Swindon. Austin Rover was very keen to dissuade Honda from using Swindon as a manufacturing facility. Quite apart from concern about the commercial leverage this would give when we were negotiating the terms for the supply of the vehicles which we were to build for them, we also had a lot of spare capacity. The most recent Corporate

Plan had come to the inescapable conclusion that Cowley South Works would have to be closed. This did provide an opportunity to offer Honda the use of the facility and thus avoid closure. Project Jupiter, as it was codenamed, was seriously discussed with and considered by Honda, but in the end, they could not make any commercial sense out of a project to build a unique vehicle for themselves, at relatively low volumes, which would require high investment due to the need for very substantial levels of local content. This also applied to their own Swindon plant and so the question of vehicle build there also went onto the back burner for the time being.

Third was the question of where to build R8/YY, Honda having a preference for Cowley, whereas the Austin Rover plan was for Longbridge. Honda were very concerned about the Cowley situation and did their best to persuade us to build R8/YY, or at least their version there, rather than at Longbridge. There was a variety of reasons for this preference of theirs. I suspect that they were concerned that they might be blamed in some way by the public for the Cowley closure, but it also always appeared to me that they were more comfortable with Cowley-based projects than Longbridge ones. This persisted throughout the relationship, but I cannot give a reason for it. They did however accept the commercial logic supporting the Longbridge decision when this was explained to them.

Into the middle of these complex strategic discussions, and alongside our R8/YY and XX problems, a bombshell suddenly dropped. In late September, three key members of the Austin Rover Board departed very suddenly: Harold Musgrove, Chairman and Chief Executive; Mark Snowdon, Managing Director (Product Development); and Peter Regnier, Director of Finance Planning (Product Development). Harold's departure was not a great surprise. It had been clear from the beginning that there was a fundamental personality clash between Graham Day and him, and Graham was the boss. The departure of Mark and Peter was much more of a surprise. On a personal basis, Mark had been my boss for several years and, although regarded by some as difficult to get on with, he and I had a good, comfortable working relationship.

We were in the middle of a round of meetings with Honda. Mr Ishikawa, by this time Executive Vice-President, was in the UK to progress discussions on the subjects outlined above, as well as the commercial negotiations about engines for R8/YY. The team on our side was Mike Carver, Mark Snowdon, David Puckering (who worked with me), and myself. We had one day of discussions. Mr Ishikawa was going to Belgium for the following day and so we arranged to have a one-day break before reconvening at Hobart Place in London. In the evening we all had dinner together, after which I went home to the Midlands on the train, having arranged to meet Mark in the office at Canley at 8.00 am on the following morning. I duly arrived at the office for our get together, but there was no Mark. As he had stayed the night in London and was being driven up first thing, I assumed that he had been held up in traffic. Eventually my direct line rang and it was Mark. In response to my joking: "where the hell are you, I've been here for hours?" he just replied that he was in the car, on his way home and would call me from there and explain. By the time he rang again, we had been formally told the news and had met the new management team of Les Wharton, Managing Director, Austin Rover; Chris Woodwark, Commercial Director, Austin Rover; and Tony Rose, Finance Director, Rover Group. These posts were not exact replacements for the ones vacated by Mark, Harold and Peter. In my role of Director of Product & Business Strategy, I now reported to Les Wharton and became a member of the enlarged Austin Rover Group Board.

Honda had been informed of the changes and we carried on with the follow-up meeting as previously planned. They had become familiar with our particular speciality of management change by upheaval, but this had been rather abrupt, even by our standards. We were now very much in a new management era. It was quite clear that Graham's early comment about the value which he placed on the Honda relationship was seriously meant, and that the business strategy and direction of the relationship would come much more from the centre than before. As a result I effectively had two bosses; Les Wharton, Managing Director of Austin Rover Group, was my full-time boss; but for strategic Honda matters it was really Mike Carver, who was on the Board of Rover Group, to whom I would look for direction.

It all worked well and a good working relationship soon got established. Mike had, of course, been deeply involved in the relationship from the start and so we had always got on. The situation was more comfortable now that the balance of power and authority at the centre was more clearly defined. The first step was to bring Les Wharton up to speed, because there were a lot of complicated and difficult things going on which were absolutely Austin Rover's responsibility; like getting XX properly launched, building Ballades and Legends, and pressing on with R8/YY. On this latter one we were getting close to the completion of the Design & Development Agreement, and a Heads of Agreement on manufacturing the cars. It was also at about this time that Honda told us that they were thinking of doing a 4-door booted version of YY.

Rover Group was in the throes of another Corporate Plan review, as the situation on the car front in particular, was serious. The plans for the closure of Cowley South continued but there was, even so, concern that we would still have more capacity than we needed. Discussions with Honda continued on Project Jupiter, and despite the unsatisfactory financial status and uncertainty about the future, the subject of possible Honda equity participation continued to be discussed. The situation was a difficult one, Rover Group was very keen to get Honda's agreement in principle to them taking an equity stake, if possible before any other action on privatisation for Austin Rover, as this would be a significant attraction for potential institutional investors. Honda, while not rejecting the idea, would not give any commitments while the future of the company was uncertain and no one could give them any idea of price and timing.

They also seemed at this time a little uncertain about their own future strategy in Europe. The economics of manufacturing vehicles unique to them, either themselves or by Austin Rover on their behalf, were not making commercial sense at their forecast volume levels, particularly given the level of investment required to meet local content requirements. They were interested in the possibility of using Cowley South, but were very concerned about getting involved with a labour force which had not been trained in the Honda way. What they really wanted was to produce cars in a nice, new, uncompromised and untainted Honda plant at Swindon. They were very keen to avoid employing people at Swindon who had previously worked in other car factories, as they would need to be de-trained before being re-trained in the Honda Way. Nevertheless, there did seem to be a concern on their part that they would have problems if Cowley South closed and they subsequently started building at Swindon. For our part we would very much have liked to have used our excess capacity to build cars for them and to have avoided the generation of additional capacity at Swindon. By this time however Nissan was the Prime Minister's favourite car company and Toyota were talking seriously about coming to the UK. The Government could not take a negative line with Honda when they expressed the wish to manufacture here, even if they had wanted to.

At the same time all the other subjects were still under active discussion, negotiation, and fighting over, as usual. We reached the stage by December that the R8/YY Development & Design Agreement could be signed, together with a Heads of Agreement on manufacturing arrangements. This Agreement was much simpler than its predecessor on XX, as basic design responsibility was with Honda R&D to a much greater extent than on XX. Problems were beginning to develop around the build quality of the sub-contract cars, ie the Legends and Ballades which we built for Honda. This was the start of a running battle which, to some degree, continued up to the final runout of the last Concerto built at Longbridge. We had problems on both vehicles, but far more on Legend. This was where the culture difference really came into play. It also created internal difficulties between Austin Rover and the parent company, Rover Group.

Nevertheless, some other aspects of the relationship were becoming clearer. We confirmed to Honda that R8/YY build would be at Longbridge and not Cowley as they preferred. The K-series engine programme was going ahead at full steam. Despite all the traumas of 1986, and all the problems which we had, things did seem to be moving in roughly the right direction at the end of the year.

Chapter 12
1987: THE YEAR OF QUALITY!
Damn Yankees - or why must the Americans be so difficult?

With the start of sub-contract build for Honda, the relationship entered a new phase. Until now, Honda had not involved themselves seriously in Austin Rover's quality situation. The cars which we had built for ourselves in collaboration with them were largely their design, and had sufficient supply of key quality critical components to ensure that they developed a very good reputation for quality in the market, in contrast to the in-house product of that time; and anyway, they had Rover badges on them. Now that they were confronted with the Austin Rover build quality arriving at the Swindon Pre-delivery Inspection (PDI) facility with a Honda badge on it, they were not happy.

Quality at British Leyland had always been, and remained, a problem. To some of us, one of the great potential benefits from the relationship was the opportunity to learn from Honda, most particularly in this area. The attitude internally had generally been one that the new products, combined with the resolution of labour relations disputes, would solve the problem. There had been a positive rejection of the idea that we could, should, and desperately needed to learn from Honda. Time went by and Metro, Maestro and Montego had, in succession, demonstrated that the quality achievement was certainly not improving sufficiently. Likewise, on many areas of XX design there had been disagreement, and what should have been common components became unique, with Austin Rover designing its own, which was a contributing factor. By the middle of 1985 this message was beginning to be recognised in Austin Rover, but with some reluctance. The problem was identified to some extent, the solution was unclear. In what was a 'management by bullying' culture, when the shouting didn't give the required result, everyone became a little unsure about what to do.

The whole subject could be expounded on at length but enough has been said to set the scene. Early in 1987, Honda started to apply major pressure on the whole quality issue. In particular, on R8/YY they insisted on having much more control over design and build quality standards, and also that Austin Rover must accept a Technical Assistance Programme to support the pre-launch and early production phase of the build. Austin Rover was starting its own in-house Total Quality Impact (TQI) programme which was to lay the foundations for the change in attitudes which would so improve the company. Because of this, and because it would cost money, the Honda position was not wholeheartedly welcomed within Austin Rover. Fortunately, it *was* welcomed at the centre by the parent company Rover Group and the wheels were put in motion which eventually saw the R8 launched at a quality level which took it right to the top of the European quality tree. The Technical Assistance Programme, combined with Austin Rover's own efforts stimulated by the TQI initiative, began to deliver. In early 1987, however, that conclusion was a long way off and there were some very heated meetings about quality. The Austin Rover manufacturing management was particularly offended by Honda's complaints and criticisms and much internal time was spent arguing that Honda were being unreasonable in their demands, or that they couldn't sell the cars and wanted to cut back supply. In fact, Honda's criticisms and constructive proposals were usually well made and, under pressure, changes were brought about.

Regardless of all this, we pressed ahead and got the final R8/YY Agreements, including the one for Technical Assistance, signed at the end of April. During one of the meetings held that year between Graham Day and Mr Kume we had what was, to me, the very essence of a company policy statement. The background was that we were, as usual, arguing over the quality of the vehicles which we were supplying. In a desperate attempt to prove that Honda were being unreasonable, the manufacturing people obtained some Honda Accords which had been built in Japan, and had them inspected by our quality audit team. Needless to say, the cars were not perfect. They were actually very good, but there were thought to be enough faults to make a case. Graham was briefed accordingly and agreed, somewhat reluctantly I felt, to raise the subject with Mr Kume. This he duly did. Mr Kume's response could not have been bettered if he had been given a detailed briefing in advance. The words he used in reply were as follows: "I know, they are terrible. The important thing is that we know that and are seriously striving to put it right. What we are trying to do is to build the perfect motor car. We recognise that it may be impossible, but we do know that if we stop trying, we are finished." There wasn't an answer to that and we moved on to other things. It remains a statement worthy of repetition and aptly demonstrates some of the attitudinal problems which still divided the two companies at that time. It was also being made about a car which was regarded by the customers as a paragon of quality virtue.

This year also saw considerable activity on the V6 engine front. The programme for the Austin Rover Zeta V6 engine, planned as a longer-term replacement for the Honda V6 and which was to be designed and developed in collaboration with Porsche Design, had now folded. It was a casualty of capital expenditure cuts necessitated by the poor profit performance. The XX Manufacturing Agreement, which covered the supply of V6 engines from Honda, had been signed in 1984. At that time Zeta had been a favoured future project in Austin Rover, and so the contractual arrangements negotiated for the Honda V6 walked a tightrope between protecting Austin Rover's security of supply, and having the right to terminate supply when and if it wanted to. It should be explained that fitting a V6 engine into the engine compartment of the XX, together with all the other essentials like air conditioning and anti-lock braking, was a triumph of squeezing a quart into a pint pot. So finding an engine which would fit from another source was extremely difficult.

So here we were in 1987, with no Zeta project and the car being prepared for launch in the USA. The USA was only interested in the V6-engined version, the 2-litre 4-cylinder version which was the European volume seller was too small an engine for a market which still liked larger engines. All the pre-launch feedback from the market was most encouraging. The American importer and distributor, a newly established joint venture with a very experienced American dealership group, was reporting a very high level of enthusiasm from the dealers. The advertising platform was that this was the car which gave you the best of both worlds, Honda quality and reliability coupled with traditional British style and image. It was a combination which, if successful, would have given Mercedes and BMW cause for concern in the US market.

Honda America was seriously concerned. There had been a preference for the Rover style on the part of the US Honda management, and so the combination of this with the sales platform and very competitive pricing, made them fairly vocal in their complaints to Tokyo. The result of all this was that Austin Rover became seriously concerned about the long-term security of supply and volume availability on the V6 engine, as the pressure was rapidly building up from the American distribution company for much higher volumes than originally forecast, together with the addition of a coupe derivative to provide even more volume.

Honda was normally very receptive to requests for higher volume supply on components as it obviously meant profitable business to them. In this case however there was a concern that pressure from Honda America might cause them to take a less enthusiastic approach to supporting the growth of a related competitor. The Legend, and the separate Acura sales network which Honda had established to sell their up-market products, was having a considerable success in the USA. This did not, however, ease Honda America's initial worries about this new kid on the block. In order to get the situation clarified, we wrote to Mr Ishikawa, asking him for assurance that Honda would be able to supply us with a substantially higher volume of V6 engines for a longer period than was provided for in the original agreement. Our forecasts were for about 60,000 units a year, or 70,000 if the coupe went ahead. His response was to say that 60,000 was all right but they would have to study whether 70,000 was achievable from the existing production capacity. It is very sad to have to record that within a few months I was negotiating the revised supply contract, and fighting to try to avoid penalty clauses if the actual volume was less than 25,000 units a year (it was substantially less).

The whole story of the Legend and the Sterling in the USA merits a complete write-up on its own. From Rover Group's point of view, it was a major tragedy and the only benefit which came from it was the absolute confirmation of the message that, on matters related to quality, it was extremely foolish to ignore Honda's advice. In the end, we finished up with the nightmare situation where the two sister cars appeared in the *J D Power's Customer Satisfaction Index*, which was a nationwide survey of owner's opinions of their cars given much publicity in the USA. The Legend was Number 1, the Sterling was either last or next to last. The reason was brutal but simple; the parts on the Sterling which caused the problems were, to a very great extent, the ones engineered uniquely by Rover, not infrequently in disagreement with Honda. This combined with less-than-ideal production processes, problems with spare parts supply, and dealer communication problems, to create a situation in the unforgiving US market which eventually led to an ignominious withdrawal. Some of the quality problems were of course also present in the Honda Legends being built at Cowley, and so there were major battles over the acceptance standards for the cars.

When the R8/YY Agreements were signed in Tokyo in April, it had been done against a background of insistence from Honda that they should be far more directly involved in the quality delivery of the project, but also against a jointly recognised need to review where the relationship was going. Honda had experienced management upheaval within Rover Group, talk about privatisation, a frequently difficult operating relationship, quality performance which did not meet their requirements on the cars Austin Rover were building for them, and the example of their two major competitors, Toyota and Nissan, establishing their own factories in the UK.

Rover Group was very aware of Honda's wish to develop some degree of independence from them, this was coupled with recognition that independent privatisation would be much more difficult without a strong link with Honda. At the same time there were strongly held views in parts of Rover that Honda used their position to negotiate deals more favourable to them than to us. The truth was that Honda did, of course, make money out of the components and equipment supplied to Austin Rover. Conversely, Austin Rover did, for a long while, get good value and very high-quality supplies. At the same time, they were failing to take advantage of the learning potential freely available from Honda. It all added up to a need for some serious discussion.

To get this started a meeting was arranged in Toronto in July. As far as I can recall, Toronto was chosen because various people were in North America on other business at the time, and anyway it made a change from Japan or the UK. The Honda party comprised Mr Ishikawa, Kiyoshi Ikemi, Shuko Hayashi (the usual team) plus Mr Osamu Iida, a member of the Honda Board who was to be responsible for commercial matters with us. The Rover Group team was led by Mike Carver with Les Wharton, Frances Elliot (Government Relations Executive) and myself. From the outset it was agreed that the privatisation of Austin Rover was probably at least three years away and the Honda position regarding a possible shareholding was understood. It was not therefore an item for the agenda. The items discussed were various, however the main events which come to mind were related to XX. Firstly, they advised us that they would not want to handle the replacement car as a joint programme. The reasons which they gave for this decision were reasonable and logical. What it boiled down to was that the investment required for build in the UK, at the level of local content required and at the then Yen/£ exchange rate, did not make commercial sense at the potential volume levels.

This completely logical approach then led to the statement that it would not now be possible to achieve satisfactory levels of local sourcing on the current Legend model, and that therefore they would like us to cease manufacture of it when we started YY production for them at Longbridge. By this time there was so much difficulty about getting the Cowley-built Legends to a quality level acceptable to Honda that this proposal was seen as constructive rather than a problem. In addition, Austin Rover was certainly not in a position to replace the Rover 800 as soon as Honda were planning to replace the Legend, particularly as the implication was that Honda were planning not to have very much carryover from the XX to the new model. Eventually, over the next 12 months, we negotiated the new Agreements which terminated the build of the Legend at Cowley and the Sterling at Sayama, together with the terms for the long-term supply of the Honda-supplied components which we needed, such as the V6 engines.

Discussions were also started with the objective of identifying what, if anything, should be the next joint product programme after R8/YY. There were no conclusions at this meeting, other than the confirmation that it wouldn't be the replacement for Rover 800/Legend. This suited us both for different reasons; we didn't want the investment of a full replacement programme on Rover 800 at this time, and Honda wanted to do it on their own. They did mention that they were thinking seriously about doing a 4-door version of the YY for themselves in Japan. This was not a surprise as the Japanese market was then not keen on the European 5-door hatchback body style typified by the R8/YY. They wanted a booted saloon. Part of the agreements on all these joint projects was that we would talk to one another about derivative models, with a view to establishing whether joint action was feasible or desirable. In this instance Honda was told straight away that we were not interested, as we had already got the 3-door model in the range, unique to Austin Rover, and didn't need a 4-door.

To understand the subsequent product actions, it is necessary to explain the status of the Austin Rover product plan at this stage. Under the previous management regime, Austin Rover's priority programme after R8/YY was AR6, a completely new and larger replacement for Metro. This was an in-house project, independent of Honda, and required very high investment. The financial situation was such that, at the time of the management change, the AR6 was an early casualty. It was replaced by R6, which installed the new K-Series power unit into the Metro, which was rebranded Rover and had a revision to the front end of the car. There was to be a facelift for Rover 800, which eventually turned into the major changes to the front and rear end which, together with a substantial sorting out the original quality problems, created the version which stayed in production up to 1998/9. Finally, there was a plan to make a Rover car to fill the gap between R8 and Rover 800 which would supplant the very 'Austin' Montego. This project was designated R9 and was to be a 4-door saloon built on a lengthened R8 platform. Honda had always insisted that they would not give us access to the Accord, which was the type of car needed to fill that product gap. The existence of the R9 project was the reason for the very rapid rejection of any involvement in the proposed 4-door YY project.

1987 continued, with further meetings both internal and between the companies. The quality issues remained, but were now being treated in a more positive manner than before and things were improving. The R8/YY project was gaining momentum and the project teams were operating in a far more effective and constructive manner than they had on XX. It was certainly not all sweetness and light, it never could be, but the allocation of responsibilities on R8/YY, with Honda R&D responsible for most of the design and development on the 5-door and 4-door cars, was far more workable than the shared responsibilities on XX. Crucially, it also made the retention of the required level of commonality between the Rover and Honda versions much easier to achieve.

Mike Bryant came in from Ford to take on the new job of Project Director and the team was enlarged and strengthened. Tribute must be paid to the team, who stuck with the project and, despite the great difficulties, delivered a product which was very successful, went to the top of the European quality tables and played a substantial role in the eventual change in the public perception of the company. The internal Honda view was that Rover had got a better product out of the deal than Honda.

The new management team at Austin Rover did have problems adjusting to the frequently uncomfortable facts of life about the relationship with Honda. It would have made life much simpler and more comfortable for everyone if Austin Rover could have been successful on its own, without any Honda involvement. Unfortunately, life wasn't like that, but acceptance of that fact was never easy; the second half of 1987 and the first half of 1988 probably represented the most protracted period of uncertainty about the relationship up to that time. The attitude at the centre was different. There was a clear recognition that a healthy Honda relationship would greatly support the privatisation of Austin Rover, which was considered a major priority.

We also had a change of heart about the 4-door version of the R8/YY. Having told Honda that we were not interested earlier in the year we now changed our minds and told them we wanted to join in. The reason for this change was simple; initially Austin Rover had been concerned that a 4-door R8 would damage the case for the larger R9. It was now clear that the R9 project was unlikely to ever be approved and so a 4-door R8 would help plug the gap. Although Honda had appeared to be quite upset when we originally said no, they were not particularly enthusiastic now that we had changed our minds. This was certainly a negotiating stance, as they did want the car in Europe, and that only made sense if we built it for them alongside the Honda 5-door. Nevertheless, they made us work for their agreement to us having access to the design for ourselves.

What had happened was that they had steamed ahead on their own when we had said no, and had started to develop the car for the Japanese market. By the time we told them that we were interested they had already commenced development of the project. This enabled them to insist that we pay a royalty for the 4-door, unlike the 5-door which had been treated as a joint development project with equal rights to the common design. I felt certain that if we had been involved from the beginning, we could have included it in the common programme and have had some say in the product definition. The milk was spilt and so there was no point in crying. We did a deal, and in the end the Rover 400, as the 4-door was named, became a much greater success for Rover than for Honda, particularly after the traditional radiator grille was fitted in 1992.

1987 witnessed an interesting, but unsuccessful attempt to establish a collaborative project that did not involve Honda directly. It was created by concern about our reliance on Honda for the 1.6-litre engines fitted to R8 and the commercial leverage this gave Honda in pricing negotiations on the engines. The revitalised Austin Rover engine range now had two main elements. First was the K-Series (1.1/1.4-litre). Second was the T-Series (2-litre), which was developed from M16, itself a development of the O-Series engine. These were both high performance units with twin camshafts and 4-valves per cylinder. The only way to achieve a 1.6-litre version of K-series would have involved a major investment programme for additional capacity as well as significant design changes.

An alternative strategy was therefore sought and a project called L16 was embarked on. This was effectively a twin-cam, 4-valve per cylinder version of the S-Series engine fitted in Maestro, Montego and Rover 200. The S-Series had in turn been developed from the E-Series, first introduced as a 1.5-litre unit in the Maxi in 1969. Never a very impressive engine, despite the improvements made to it, by the late 1980s it was becoming rather out of date. The attraction of the L16 route was that the basic production capacity existed in plenty, and all that was required was new cylinder head equipment and tooling. Prototype engines had been built and run with encouraging results, but the project had been cancelled because of shortage of funds, combined with the availability of the Honda 1.6-litre units for the R8/YY.

At this time Czechoslovakia still existed and was still 'the People's Republic of'. Their major motor manufacturer was Skoda and, although it was fashionable to make jokes about the cars, I had respect for their engineering heritage. We came up with the idea that, if we offered them a licence to build the L16 engine for themselves and for us, the Czechoslovakian Government might support the investment required for the engine, as it would make the Skoda cars more competitive in export markets and would also earn substantial hard currency from engine or component sales back to us. It seemed worth the attempt and so I had some discussions with the Czech Embassy, who thought enough of the idea to fix visas and appointments with an industry minister in Prague and with the Skoda people at their plant.

It turned out to be a complete anti-climax, everyone was quite interested until we got to Skoda. They were polite but cool and very definitely not interested. It was all rather a disappointment but did provide me with my first visit to an Iron Curtain country, other than the Moscow Airport transit lounge. My main memory is of being surprised by the attractiveness of Prague, and the fact that all the taxi-drivers were part-time; their main occupation seemed to be illegal currency dealing. Certainly, when you got into a cab the first question was not: "where to?" but: "do you want to change some money?"

That was the last gasp of the L16 engine project, as far as I know nothing has been preserved. Things moved on and a way was found to do the 1.6-litre (and indeed 1.8-litre) versions of K-Series, which was a much better outcome than having a unique 1.6-litre engine.

Chapter 13
1988: PRIVATISATION
A change of shareholder and much else

The year started in the usual fashion, with continuing problems about the R8 project, and discontent with our quality performance on the build of Legend and Ballade. Negotiations continued on the agreement for the 4-door R8. The atmosphere within Austin Rover was difficult. Despite the support for the relationship at the centre of Rover Group, in some parts of Austin Rover the pressure being applied by Honda was beginning to be felt and was resented. After the problems with Legend and Ballade quality, Honda had made it quite clear that the price for the continuation of the R8 project was to do things their way, and to accept assistance and advice from them.

This was really the very best thing which could have happened but it was, understandably, not universally welcomed within Austin Rover. It was, however becoming increasingly clear that any go-it-alone product programme was unlikely to receive the support of the Rover Group Board or 'The Shareholder'. The background to this situation was, of course, the escalating quality problem with the Rover 800, which was to have such a devastating effect in the USA in particular, as described already.

The discussions with Honda on future product strategy, which had started after the Toronto meeting, were moving very slowly and really didn't seem to be getting anywhere in particular. My own conclusion was that Honda wanted to be more certain of progress on the R8 project before getting themselves committed to the next step. The knock-on effect within Austin Rover, was the emergence of an equivocal attitude towards the relationship. There was an underlying attitude that the relationship could be a very good thing if only ...

The 'if only' included; doing things for us free; letting us do things our own way, even if it didn't work or was unproven; and cutting the pressure on us to do things their way. This is an exaggeration but only a bit of one. It does actually reflect some of the underlying attitudes at that time. Honda were not easy partners and we frequently had very major arguments and disagreements on both commercial and technical matters. Nevertheless, they remained our most direct route to competitive performance and, with that, our best hope of survival. It remained, however, an unwelcome and resented message in some areas, despite all the evidence.

One thing which did develop in Austin Rover was a belief that joint design and development projects like XX and R8/YY were far too expensive and difficult, and that some form of licence agreement, with Honda doing most of the engineering, was probably the best way to go in future. This attitude was driven by the general attack on costs, including cutting back on engineering expenditure. As our level of engineering spend was extremely low by competitive standards, the implications of any further reductions were pretty serious. It certainly did not support a competitive go-it-alone product plan. Licence-deals with Honda had the appeal that the royalty payments would only be made after the sale of the vehicle, thus benefitting cash flow. This was quite apart from the fact that the quality of the design could be relied on absolutely.

Although many people in Austin Rover did not agree, my own view is that the royalty charges represented good value for money. My reservations about this approach were that, although it gave us an extremely good service, it did not do very much to support and encourage the in-house skills in engineering which were so essential for the future. Although there was nothing agreed at that time regarding a project to follow after R8 - in fact there was nothing really under discussion at all on the future product front - it subsequently became clear that Honda were beginning to have similar feelings about the problems with joint engineering programmes.

Further uncertainty was thrown into the mix by Honda's announcement that Mr Ishikawa would shortly retire. Mr Ishikawa was a very senior Honda manufacturing engineer who had risen to be Executive Vice-President of Honda. He had been deeply involved with the relationship since early in 1979 and had been in a very good position to speak for the relationship within Honda. He was a good friend to Austin Rover, and his support against the 'anti' lobby within Honda (which always existed) was valued, quite apart from the constructive part which he always played in the Austin Rover scene. We were told that Mr Iida would now be our spokesman on the Honda Board in Tokyo and our main board level contact. We all liked and respected Mr Iida but were concerned that our main contact was now a fairly junior director, rather than an Executive Vice-President. In the event it didn't seem to make a great deal of difference, but it did fuel the fires of uncertainty at the time.

Mr Ishikawa left a good legacy. In the previous year, during the final negotiations on the R8/YY agreement, Honda had applied very heavy pressure to ensure that they would exercise maximum influence over the quality of the vehicles which we would build for us both; particularly the Concerto, of course. All the stops had been pulled out and the quality of the Ballades being built for them at Longbridge had already improved sufficiently for the R8/YY project to go ahead. In addition to this, Honda had 'very strongly recommended' (Japanese polite-speak for insisted) that we avail ourselves of technical assistance which they would provide. This took the form of a substantial number of their engineers and technicians, who would be based at Longbridge to assist, advise and train our people in the Honda way of preparing for the production and launch of the new cars.

This approach, which was very good news to some of us, was not universally welcomed in Austin Rover. The assistance was fine but the fact that we would have to contribute to its cost was another thing entirely. The deal which was done, with Austin Rover contributing only a third of the cost, was probably some of the best value for money any manufacturer ever received. The amount spent provided a very rapid financial return on reduced warranty costs, quite apart from the enormous benefits which came from the transformation of the company's quality image, which commenced with the launch of the new Rover 200 under this regime.

Despite the uncertainties about the future of the relationship, there was plenty happening on the operational front and so we kept pretty busy, as usual. Even so, I was aware that Mike Carver had been keeping a low profile for a few weeks. We then went out to Tokyo for a meeting where, having sworn me to secrecy, he revealed the big secret, that the whole operation was to be sold to British Aerospace. Privatisation had come and sooner than expected.

It was quite a surprise. Mike had been very involved in the deal, and Honda were fully in the picture; Lord Young, then Secretary of State for Trade and Industry, accompanied by Graham Day and Professor Rowland Smith, the British Aerospace Chairman, had met Mr Kume to give him the news and request confirmation of Honda's continued participation, which had of course been given. It was now clear that, even though things would probably be somewhat different, the new owners saw the Honda relationship as being of fundamental importance in the future of the company. The change of ownership would not change the operational difficulties inherent in such a complex relationship, but it would, hopefully, provide a more positive background than had existed recently.

It all happened and by the end of August we were part of British Aerospace and no longer a thorn in the flesh of Margaret Thatcher's Government. Nothing happened very quickly from my point of view, but in October we went off to Tokyo for a meeting between Graham Day and Mr Kume which provided the start of the transition from the old situation to the new. It soon became clear that British Aerospace did not intend to involve themselves in the operational management of the company; however, there were going to be changes.

In essence, British Aerospace had acquired Austin Rover and Land Rover, together with a shareholding in Leyland-DAF and other trade investments. Up to now, Austin Rover and Land Rover had been operated as completely separate companies. This was to change, with the two operations merged into a single Rover Group. The three separate boards of Austin Rover, Land Rover and Rover Group became one, with Graham Day as Chairman; George Simpson was brought back from Leyland-DAF as Managing Director. This all became effective in mid-January and Graham became Sir Graham in the New Year's Honours List. From now on it would be just 'Rover' not 'Austin Rover'.

This new organisation was another upheaval. From my point of view, I was not on the Rover Group Board but reported to Roland Bertodo, who had been Engineering Director of Austin Rover and was now made Strategic Planning Director for Rover Group.

A visit to Honda's Suzuka factory in 1989. From left to centre: Osamu Iida, Tony Rose, Frances Elliott, Roland Bertodo, George Simpson, Mike Carver, John Bacchus. To the right of them are Masami Suzuki and Shuko Hayashi (not in uniform) plus some of the factory workers.

Tadashi Kume and Sir Graham Day (centre) sign a Statement of Understanding in London, July 1989. John Bacchus is standing between them at the back. Rover Group and Honda affirmed their joint intention to sign a cross-shareholding arrangement along with agreements re the design and manufacture of the 'Synchro' by the end of the year.

A Honda Concerto saloon at Canley in 1988. It has a British 'E' registration plate, showing that this a very early Japanese version of the R8 which has been brought over to the UK for viewing.

A Dinoc clay model of an early Synchro styling concept (the Rover 600). It was photographed at Canley on 29 September 1989.

The Rover 200 (R8) was built at Longbridge. 'Doors off doors on' or 'DODO' was another innovative manufacturing technique. Once the bodyshell had been painted, the doors were removed to progress down their own assembly line, providing the workforce with much easier access for fitting out the interior. It also reduced the opportunity to accidentally damage the doors, which were re-united with the car near the end of the track.

The R8 was produced in two versions, the Rover 400 (left) and the Rover 200 (right). This picture provides a comparison between the two.

Rover Group manufactured the R8 Honda Concerto as well as Rover 200/400 at Longbridge. A Honda Engineering sign can be seen in the background.

Our Management Policy

1. Proceed always with ambition and youthfulness.
2. Respect sound theory, develop fresh ideas and make the most effective use of your time.
3. Enjoy your work and always brighten your working atmosphere.
4. Strive constantly for a harmonious flow of work.
5. Be ever mindful of the value of research and endeavour.

HONDA OF THE UK MANUFACTURING LTD. (HUM)
SWINDON, U.K.

In 1985 Honda set up a facility at Swindon, to be run by 'Honda of the UK Manufacturing Ltd' known as HUM. Initially it operated as a Pre-delivery Inspection Centre (PDI) where vehicles were quality checked, including those supplied by Rover Group, which was often a source of friction between the two companies. In 1989 it began engine assembly, producing 1.6-litre engines for the R8 derivatives. Finally, in 1992, it commenced the manufacture of complete vehicles. A publicity leaflet of that year stated its management philosophy with Japanese style.

Assembling engines at HUM Swindon in 1993. The power unit is being checked on an engine firing test bench to assess its performance.

Final vehicle quality checks at the end of the assembly line, HUM Swindon. This completed car was part of the first batch of Honda Accords (equivalent of the Rover 600 Synchro) to be manufactured by Honda at its own British factory.

Manufacture of the Honda Civic (equivalent of the Rover 400 HHR) at HUM Swindon, 1995.

Honda puts a Longbridge built Concerto R8 through its paces on a pavé track to uncover rattles and other defects.

In 1991 the Rover 800 was given a major facelift, codenamed R17.

A styling decision was made to re-introduce the traditional Rover grille. The success of this move took Rover Group by surprise, and it also annoyed their partners, as Honda felt they had not been told about the decision in advance, as was provided for in their joint agreements. The grille proved so popular that it would quickly be deployed across the entire Rover model range. Some owners even fitted one to their pre-facelift cars.

Chapter 14
1989: MAKING IT LEGAL AT LAST
After three children and another on the way

After the meeting between Graham Day and Mr Kume in October 1988, things had started to move again as far as the relationship was concerned. At that meeting, Mr Kume had explained his view of the future by saying that: "If the two companies could work together to develop their position in Europe, whilst maintaining their independence, then that would be a wonderful thing". After a few trips to Tokyo by early February we were beginning to get a clearer picture of where Honda's thoughts were leading them.

It was also clear that the British Aerospace Board were not happy about the informal nature of the overall relationship. They felt the need for the security of an Agreement which would link Honda more formally and, in their view, more securely to Rover. The shareholding issue was back on the table again, but this time Honda were prepared to talk seriously. They also began to expose their own thinking to us. The key element was not unexpected, they wanted to develop Honda Swindon to become a car manufacturing plant. They were thinking of building a larger car than Concerto there, probably an Accord in some form. By early spring we were into serious discussions on both the shareholding and strategic fronts.

The Shareholders' Agreement was principally the responsibility of Tony Rose, the Rover Group Director of Finance. The key issues were corporate structure and valuation. The valuation was particularly difficult, as Rover Group did not have a profit record, and the price recently paid by British Aerospace to the British Government was not an acceptable basis. Sir Graham and Mr Kume had agreed in principle that the shareholdings would be in Rover Group and Honda of the UK (Manufacturing) Ltd, referred to as HUM Swindon, and everything moved ahead on that basis.

At the same time things were beginning to move on the product front; there was a considerable amount of coming and going and much discussion around the product plan. Having had a change of management, there had to be a serious review of existing plans, and in any case there were a lot of uncertainties regarding what followed R8. The R9 project was still around but not really alive, and the eternal problem of the replacement for Metro was receiving a lot of attention but was without a solution. It had been decided to facelift the Rover 800, but it was also recognised that a replacement plan was needed. In the first half of the year things began to become clearer from the Honda end. Their plans for HUM Swindon started to firm up and led to them proposing to us that they should build a Honda, plus a Rover version, of a derivative of the scheduled 1992 model year Accord. This would be balanced by an eventual replacement programme for the R8/YY which would see the continuation of Rover building cars for Honda.

The principles were simple, the practicalities were more complicated. Rover liked these ideas, but was also very keen to talk to Honda about a collaborative project on a small car. This was not so easy. At this time, we were saying that we had to have the small car by 1993, Honda quite simply said it was much too early for them to contemplate, and anyway, they saw the 3-door Civic as filling the product need for them for the time being. We did continue to try to persuade them to consider some form of collaboration on the concept which started to develop into a vehicle based on R8 but somewhat smaller. At this stage, however, they were not interested in joining in with us. The message was also being put quite firmly that all projects from now on would be based on a licensed build approach, Honda R&D had had enough of joint design and development projects, even when they were in the driving seat as on R8/YY. This was very much in line with Rover's wish to get the maximum benefit from Honda R&D's involvement. The question of paying for it was, however, to remain a major issue from here on.

There was also a lot of discussion on the subject of the large car strategy. Honda were at this time well into their project for the Legend replacement. They had only recently given us the really important information about the car. This was that, although it was to remain front-wheel drive, the engine would be mounted longitudinally rather than transversely as in the XX. Our initial reaction to this was that it sounded very intriguing and we might be interested in using the platform for a replacement Rover 800 programme. Honda were quite happy to talk about this, and for a very brief period we contemplated a replacement Rover 800 which would use our own style on the Honda platform design, continuing to use the (new) Honda V6 engine at the top of the range and our own 2-litre petrol and diesel engines for the bulk of the volume. Very quickly, however, a small problem emerged. In a very elegant piece of design, the final drive to the front wheels passed through the engine crankcase, which meant that the engine had to be designed that way in the first place. There was no way in which our smaller engines could be adapted for installation in the FS, as the new Legend was designated; and so, despite much investigation, the idea never developed.

Because of the ever-present risk of leaks, it was agreed mid-year, that we would set up and sign a Statement of Understanding which would outline what we were talking about. The outline could then be released to the media and we could get on with the detailed agreements. It would also allow Honda to go ahead with the development of the HUM facility at Swindon for the manufacture of cars. Production was just starting there on the engines required to support the R8/YY early build at Longbridge.

The principles of the cross-shareholding were sufficiently agreed to enable the intention to be announced, Tony Rose having settled a deal in principle which effectively valued the part of Rover Group in which Honda would have a shareholding at £520 million. The investment in HUM, when it was completed, would be £370 million. The final position which Tony agreed was reciprocal 20% shareholdings plus a £30 million cash payment from Honda. The Statement of Understanding was completed in quite a rush and was signed in London in mid-July, the stated intention being to sign both the cross-shareholding and the 'Synchro' Agreements by the end of the year. Synchro was the code name given to the project for the cars to be built for us both at HUM Swindon. The press and media reaction was generally good; the full details of the shareholding arrangement had been played down in the information released. No-one picked up the point that British Aerospace had received, in cash and shares, £104 million for 20% of less than the whole company, for which they had paid £150 million only 11 months previously.

The whole affair culminated in a joint press conference at the Grand Connaught Rooms in London with Sir Graham and Mr Kume in the joint chairs. We had actually celebrated the previous evening with a very convivial dinner at Claridge's Hotel with both teams in good form. Behind the scenes of course we were having the usual battles. The Shareholders' Agreement was fairly straightforward, however everything else was a fair battleground. At about this time Honda advised us that they were establishing a European Headquarters in the UK. Mr Iida would be the President, Honda Motors Europe, with my old friend and sparring partner, Shuko Hayashi, as his Director of Rover Liaison. There was concern that this establishment might weaken our links to Tokyo and Honda R&D in Tochigi, as Honda Europe were to provide the communication channel on the collaborative projects.

We did briefly have a slightly difficult situation in that there was no-one for George Simpson to directly interface with for formal discussions. This situation soon righted itself, as Mr Kawamoto started to reappear in the relationship. We had known Mr Kawamoto for a long time but he had not been directly involved with us for some time past. As an ex-President of Honda R&D, and now a Senior Managing Director, he was clearly the heir apparent to Mr Kume. I had always found him very agreeable; however, he was very much an engineer's engineer, and had in the past been more than a little critical of some of our engineering efforts. His commitment to the relationship was, to us, an unknown quantity. It was, nevertheless, nice to see him back involved in a leading role, I took it as encouraging that he now felt that things were moving in a direction which had his support.

Things started to move after the signing of the Statement of Understanding, and in early August we had a Simpson/Kawamoto meeting in Tochigi which set the scene for the new phase in the relationship. John Towers, at this time Product Development Director, was in the party and this was really the first time that Rover expressed a serious intention to learn from Honda. Synchro was beginning to become clearer and we were putting some flesh on the bones. I have to say that to me, at this stage, it was a project with very little appeal. Basically, I was unhappy that we were not building the car ourselves;

without that it seemed to me that the car would do much more for the dealer network and HUM than for Rover Group. It was not a popular position to take in Rover at the time and so, having had my say, I got on with it. The Rover Project Team was set up and my old friend Fred Coultas was appointed Project Director.

The work very quickly got underway and a team of engineers and stylists went to Tochigi to start work on the Rover identity aspects of what was to become the Rover 600. This period also saw the preparation for the launch phase of R8/YY, now settled as Rover 200 and Concerto. We had finished build of the Ballades for Honda in April, and were due to start Rover 200 in August and Honda Concerto in September. HUM Swindon were to start engine production in July. For such a complex project it all went well, including the launch of the new K-Series engine, which was so important to Rover. The combination of the Rover people with the Honda Technical Assistance Team working together was very effective, and resulted in a level of quality at the launch which was very high indeed by European standards. Honda senior management even expressed themselves impressed with the standard reached on the Concerto (though this did not prevent major running battles on the subject at the operational level).

Everyone concerned in the delivery of the programme had good reason to be pleased with the result, and this was reinforced when Mr Kawamoto paid a visit to Rover Group's Research and Proving facility at Gaydon in the early Autumn. John Towers used this visit to introduce him to a number of the research people at Gaydon, and also laid on for him a driving session in some Rover 200s, Concertos and the about-to-be-launched Discovery. His comments after the visit were very encouraging, particularly given his earlier reservations about our engineering capability. He stated quite positively that the K-Series engined Rover 200 was the nicest car in the R8/YY range. He was also impressed by the engineers he met and spoke to during the visit.

The only slightly down note was the Discovery. The one which he drove was a diesel version and, when I asked him for his opinion, he replied that he was sure it was very good but that it wasn't his type of vehicle. This was not a surprise as Honda R&D had always been very anti-diesel engine, taking the quite reasonable view that they really belonged in large merchant ships and heavy trucks. Mr Kawamoto was a great car enthusiast, particularly for sporting cars, and was the driving force behind the Honda Formula One programme. On that front he told me at dinner one evening that he saw one of the major benefits flowing from the racing programme to be the stimulation which it gave to his young engineers in R&D; this was quite as important as the direct publicity benefit.

Needless to say, there were still plenty of things for us to talk about on R8/YY. One of the less successful aspects of the car was the cost level, and a lot of time had been spent jointly during the year addressing this problem.

A programme had been set up to reduce costs, however this would take time, particularly as the hard-won quality standard could not be put at risk. The well known 'Murphy's Law' had been applied and Yen/£ exchange rates all went the wrong way as well. This all added up to a major problem on the transfer pricing for the Concertos which we were building for Honda. This was the price at which we sold the vehicles to Honda for them to sell on through their sales network. Since the two cars (Rover 200 & Concerto) became competitors as soon as they got into the showrooms, this was anyway a complicated business. When the costs were high and the exchange rates were wrong, it all became even more difficult. Eventually a compromise was agreed which did provide a reasonable balance for both companies. Peter McVeigh, who worked with me, became the ultimate expert on the whole complex operation and its control. The experience did, however, reinforce my concerns and lack of enthusiasm for the Synchro project, where we would be buying the finished cars from Honda.

There were other problems. One of these related to the equipment which Honda Engineering had supplied for the construction of the body shell. This was very specialised and very expensive equipment which welded together the sheet metal pieces making up the complete body shell. This had to be done at great speed and with great accuracy. There was a problem with the R8/YY; the quality was all right but the production rate was not up to specification. The battle started; we said that it was Honda's fault, they had designed and manufactured the equipment. They claimed that there was nothing wrong with the equipment, we had signed off its commissioning trials, we weren't operating it properly. In the end a deal was done and an intermediate operation and equipment was installed which solved the problem. Honda either paid for this or contributed significantly to the cost, I can't remember which. I still don't know who was right and who was wrong.

Mr Kume came over in October to attend the official opening of Honda's Swindon manufacturing facility, and a meeting was held between him and Sir Graham during his visit. Among other things this confirmed the arrangements which were being made for a senior management meeting regime to handle the relationship. This answered the concerns which we had about our links with Tokyo, as the idea was that this group would meet regularly and would be led by Mr Shoichiro Irimajiri, Executive Vice-President of Honda who represented the technical aspects of the business – ie development, manufacturing, manufacturing engineering and so on. Mr Kawamoto would also be a part of this team. Mr Irimajiri would face off to George Simpson who was then Managing Director of Rover. Mr Irimajiri had spent a lot of time in the USA with Honda and spoke very fluent English. Having been deeply involved with the setting up and running of Honda's car plants in the USA, he had an ability to understand our attitudes and see solutions to problems which sometimes escaped some of his colleagues. His appearance in the picture marked a significant step in improving the operating relationships between the companies. It was also fortuitous that he and John Towers established a particularly good personal relationship which subsequently was a great help in progressing the learning-from-Honda initiative in Rover.

We were moving towards finalising the Shareholders' Agreement but it wasn't ready for signature yet. Things on the Synchro front were not so encouraging, however. Although it was developing nicely in the styling/engineering area, we were having some difficulty making financial sense of the project. Again, the issue of transfer prices raised its head. There were also several other issues related to the draft Agreement which were signalling the way in which Honda would want to operate the project, and with which we were not happy. As ever, the Agreement was a legalised operating agreement rather than a legal agreement. We fought on, with us telling Honda that we would have to withdraw from the project if we couldn't make more financial sense of it.

By this time most of the discussions were going on with Mr Iida who was the President-Elect of Honda Motor Europe, which was now looking for a home in the UK. The situation was quite difficult, as the whole strategy regarding HUM Swindon, and hence the Shareholders' Agreement, only made sense if the Synchro project could be delivered. Even Honda's Synchro volume forecasts for their own version, excluding the Rover variant, did not provide a justification for the development of Swindon as a car plant. On this note of uncertainty, the year approached its end.

Chapter 15
1990: EASTER IN NEW YORK
New managements and new projects

The deliberations over the Christmas/New Year period caused some easing of the Rover hard line on Synchro to the extent that we stopped threatening to walk away; however, the problem still remained. The Shareholders' Agreement was getting very close to completion.

The key outstanding issues were down to two things. First was Honda's wish to have the right of first refusal should British Aerospace wish to sell off any more of Rover. This was eventually solved by not having it in the agreement, but by having a letter from British Aerospace assuring Honda that they would consult with them before taking any such step.

Second was Honda's wish to include the financial arrangements in the Agreement and to be prepared to have them revealed. British Aerospace were very sensitive to this at this time. The European Commission had decided that it was not at all happy about the terms on which the Government had sold Rover to British Aerospace, and an investigation was in hand on the whole subject. Eventually it was accepted that the Stock Exchange rules made it impossible to hide the information.

Because of the publicity which was surrounding the investigation by the European Commission, Honda were quite keen not to have any further publicity on the subject until after the Commission's findings had been published and any resulting reaction had time to die down. We consequently slowed down on the finalisation. There were plenty of other things to get on with. The large car issue was back in discussion, with Honda really trying very hard to be helpful. In the end, however, the same problem as before frustrated the issue. The Honda platforms which were most suitable to provide the basis for a replacement of the Rover 800, were ones designed around Honda's longitudinal installation 5-cylinder and V6 power units. We had to be able to use our own 2-litre engine and, increasingly, the market need to install a diesel engine was (regrettably) unarguable. Neither of these fundamental requirements was feasible with the Honda longitudinal layout and so, in the end, we had to give up. Honda understood and, to help out, agreed to keep the 2.7-litre V6 going for us at pretty low volume after they stopped using it, through to 1996 at least. In that year the Honda V6 engine was at last replaced by a new Rover K-Series V6.

Once the European Commission review was completed, there was a flurry of publicity about the advantageous terms under which British Aerospace had acquired Rover Group. Once this had died down a bit it was agreed that the Shareholders' Agreement should now be signed. There were still many things to be sorted out on the Synchro front and so we built a reference to it into the Shareholders' Agreement and pressed on.

Because the final decision to get it signed was made late, there were diary problems getting Sir Graham and Mr Kume together. The result was that we arranged for the meeting and signature to take place in New York during Easter weekend. This would also reduce the level of media attention to the event. I flew out with John Pullen, our Communications Director. John and I had been keeping very close to make sure that the Honda, Rover and British Aerospace public relations approaches were all co-ordinated. We were both good smokers at that time and so we happily sat together chatting and blowing smoke on one another.

On the approach into Kennedy Airport, I looked out of the window and noticed a DC10 flying parallel with us, on a similar heading and altitude. We carried on chatting for a couple of minutes and I looked again. We weren't flying on a parallel course, it was definitely a convergent one. John had been an RAF pilot and he didn't seem unduly concerned. I maintained a rigid upper lip and kept a watch on the DC10 out of the corner of my eye as we carried on with our conversation. After a few moments, during which it became distinctly larger, the DC10 suddenly broke away from us in a steep turning climb. I have always believed that Air Traffic Control at Kennedy suddenly woke up and realised that everything was not quite as it should be.

The meeting was held at the hotel where the Honda contingent were staying on Park Avenue, on the afternoon of Good Friday, 13 April. When we came to the actual signing, we ran into an unexpected problem. To our surprise, Honda revealed that they were concerned about making public that the Agreement was signed on such a significant day in the Christian calendar; the inauspiciousness of Friday the 13th was also mentioned. The solution was quickly arrived at, the documents would be signed today but undated. Kiyoshi Ikemi and I would retain them, meet on the following morning and formally date them. All I will say is that the documents were dated 14 April and how and where it actually happened is no longer relevant!

The Shareholders' Agreement was quite an unusual document. Its major function was to act as a public confirmation of the relationship. As such it made no provision for such things as dividend payments. In the event of an agreed unwinding, each party just returned to the other what it had received in the first instance. The one thing which it did contain, was a formal statement that we were one another's primary collaborative partner. Its existence did not really affect the relationship significantly; as ever, that remained rooted in a combination of commercial and strategic realities, and personal relationships.

This meeting proved to be significant for more than the signature of the Shareholders' Agreement. Mr Kume chose this opportunity to tell us that he intended to retire in the summer and that his place would be taken by Mr Kawamoto. This meant that Honda maintained their tradition of succession. Despite the fact that there were two or three Executive Vice-Presidents, Mr Kawamoto, one rung down the hierarchy, was the R&D man and thus the heir.

I liked Mr Kawamoto personally very much, but did wonder whether he would be as supportive of the relationship as his two predecessors. In the event there was no need to worry, he fully maintained the tradition of Presidential support.

After the signing and the subsequent dinner everyone departed. I was booked to leave on an evening flight on Saturday and was thus able to spend most of the day sightseeing. This was enjoyable as, despite a very busy business travelling life, it was only my second visit to New York. The first had been as a very young man with Ford in 1963.

By Autumn 1990, the new Honda management was in place and we were beginning to have management meetings with George Simpson and Mr Irimajiri leading. Further discussions and investigations took place on the large car problem. Honda tried, and we tried, but we could not come up with any way of getting to a replacement for Rover 800 which met Rover's requirements. We also continued to struggle with the Synchro commercial problems without, it must be said, making a lot of headway, and certainly without reaching a solution. We launched the R8 Rover 400 and started build of the equivalent 4-door Concerto for Honda. This of course necessitated a further round of battles on the transfer prices. The inherent problem was that Rover's strategy, which was to price the 400 above the 200, conflicted with Honda's desire to have similar pricing for the 4-door and the 5-door. We finally hammered out a solution to that one. Whilst we were going on with that lot, we also started discussions on the replacement for the Rover 200/Concerto, for which the strategic plan was that Rover would build both versions at Longbridge and the basic car would be engineered by Honda. The next questions, in order of priority were 'when?' and 'what?'

The 'when' was a bit of a problem at first, with each company having rather different views on the realistic life-cycle for the current vehicles. Honda wanted to see a replacement in early 1994. As the Concerto was not proving to be a great success in the market, this was reasonable from their point of view, and anyway nearly all Japanese-built cars were on a four-year cycle. By contrast the Rover 200/400 range had been well received by both the press and the market, and Rover had a history of excessively long model cycles. As a result, Rover had decided that it would not replace the cars until 1996. In the end a sensible compromise was agreed, with Honda going for late 1994 and Rover spring 1995.

The 'what' proved to be less of a problem. There was no serious disagreement about the general parameters for the car, which was seen as a replacement for the existing Rover 200 and Concerto. It was agreed that the core vehicle would be a joint 5-door model using both Rover and Honda engines. There was a reversal of the previous R8/YY situation in that Rover wanted a 4-door, booted version and Honda did not. It was quickly agreed that Rover would do the 4-door for itself.

This year had seen a further development in our lives. Honda Motor Europe had established itself in some very pleasant offices by the River Thames at Caversham. All of a sudden, my travelling to Japan slowed down abruptly. Driving down to Caversham was far less time-consuming and certainly saved the company a lot of money. It was a pleasant journey, partially through the lanes, and took about as long as a good journey from Narita Airport into central Tokyo. It seemed strange at the time; as far as I can tell there were only two trips to Japan in 1990, a far cry from the frenetic travelling of previous years!

The latter stages of 1990 started to become a little unsettled. Despite the Technical Assistance programme, along with serious efforts which were producing great improvements at Longbridge, it was still proving very difficult to satisfy Honda's requirements for consistency of quality and delivery on Concerto. At the same time the reaction to the Rover 200 had been far more enthusiastic than to the Honda Concerto. There was a general feeling that the relationship was about to go through one of its sticky patches. Honda was also under new management and there were noises coming from Tokyo that Mr Kawamoto intended to make some substantial changes in the way in which Honda was run.

Changes were also underway in Rover. Andy Barr, the Manufacturing Director had departed to run one of the British Aerospace companies and John Towers had been appointed as Managing Director for Product Supply, combining his Product Development role with Manufacturing and Purchase. John now started to have a more significant role in the relationship with Honda. He pushed the need for, and the opportunity to learn from Honda with an enthusiasm which had not always been evident in the past. This whole process was assisted by the very good relationship which he was developing with Mr Irimajiri.

We finished the year with a meeting between Sir Graham Day and Mr Kawamoto, which was held on a Saturday in December at the Goring Hotel in London Victoria. This was not a comfortable meeting. I had been alerted in advance that Mr Kawamoto intended to speak seriously at the meeting. He did! The core of his message was that he had concerns about Rover's determination to do what was necessary quickly enough. He was also extremely concerned about what he saw as the very leisurely Rover product programme, which did not provide any really new product, as opposed to facelifts, until the Rover Synchro started in early 1993. It was all put very politely but firmly, pointing out that Honda was relying on Rover for supplies of the Concerto, which was to be a foundation stone of their European strategy, and in addition they were significant shareholders in the company. As they had to reflect Rover's financial results in their consolidated financial report, this was a legitimate concern. This all combined with the early signs of recession and lower sales to provide for a challenging new year.

Chapter 16
1991: THE 'S-K' PROJECTS
More management changes, the Simpson/Kawamoto era

As the year started it soon became clear that change was in the air again. We were not progressing with the Synchro Agreements, although by this time we had agreed that there would be a separate Agreement to cover the supply of body components at HUM Swindon for both versions of Synchro. There was a lot of activity on the manufacturing and quality fronts and the new business unit structure was getting established. The R8/Concerto replacement had been codenamed Theta and initial work was getting underway, providing the product definition and early styling exercises with the teams in Japan. Sometime in March, George Simpson had a meeting on his own in Tokyo with Mr Kawamoto.

This was a very important meeting, because this was when the first indications were given that Honda wanted to change the plans established in the Statement of Understanding. The result of this meeting was that we very quickly got together, and a Statement of Intent was thrashed out and signed in April. This document identified the fundamental change that we would stop building cars for one another. We would continue with Concerto build for Honda until its replacement was ready, but we would each build our own versions of Synchro and Theta, sharing the costs of the common tooling. Honda R&D would remain responsible for the basic design and development programmes. Honda also agreed, in principle, to provide Rover with R&D assistance on other programmes.

This all seemed a very good thing to me. On Synchro in particular, the greater freedom of action which had to come with the build of the car was highly desirable. It was, nevertheless, a very major change to our plans and at a late stage as far as Synchro was concerned. February 1993 was the date which had been set to begin production of the Rover version at HUM Swindon. It was very quickly agreed that a basic objective was to keep that timing, even though the Rover version would now be built elsewhere. The very first decision which had to be made was where that would be. It was quickly agreed that Cowley was the most logical and suitable place for Synchro, but by this time there were only about 21 months left and an awful lot of work needed to be done by the production engineers. It was also being kept absolutely confidential at this stage; only a limited number of people in both companies were aware of what was going on and they were sworn to secrecy.

In the middle of all this our HQ had moved offices from Canley to Bickenhill (adjacent to Birmingham Airport) and I was now reporting to John Towers. It must be said that the changes to the plan were not all that welcome in Rover. Yet again they were seen as Honda taking steps to distance itself. In the short term, there was also an increased investment requirement for Synchro build, which had not been provided for in the latest Corporate Plan. This was most unwelcome, despite the fact that the additional investment required to build the car actually gave a very high profit return. There was more discussion and it was agreed that the future should be mapped out in a more definitive way than in the Statement of Intent, and so we embarked upon the drafting of a detailed Memorandum of Understanding.

Whilst this was going on, Mr Iida departed, his position as President of Honda Motor Europe being filled by Mr Shojiro Miyake who was Vice-President of Manufacturing Europe. Mr Iida's departure was quite a surprise and, as ever, was never explained, either on or off the record. Whether he had been too closely identified with the previous plan we will probably never know. All of us at Rover were sorry to see him go, as he had been a firm but agreeable collaborative partner.

The changes on the human front continued. Mr Kawamoto was pushing ahead with the organisational changes which he had started in Honda, with the emphasis on regional responsibility. Meanwhile, Sir Graham Day relinquished the chairmanship of Rover Group to become Chairman of British Aerospace. George Simpson now became Chairman of Rover and soon appointed John Towers as Group Managing Director. All of this meant that the signing of the Memorandum of Understanding took place against a background of change in both Rover and Honda.

One recognition of the new situation was that the product programmes in the Memorandum of Understanding were, at Mr Kawamoto's suggestion, given 'SK' designations as code numbers. The letters standing for Simpson-Kawamoto. It did also help that two letter codes starting with 'S' were a common project identification in Honda R&D. The designations were:

- SK1 - Synchro, became Rover 600/Honda Accord
- SK2 - Rover engined versions of SK1
- SK3 - Smaller car based on R8 platform
- SK4 - Theta, R8/YY replacement which became HHR
- SK5 - Large car project (Rover 800 replacement)

This all provided a pretty high level of activity with Honda in many parts of the company. There still remained, in some areas of Rover management, a concern that Honda were actually trying to distance themselves from Rover in preparation for a total disengagement.

I could not understand this concern, because the Memorandum of Understanding and the projects listed above, included things which had no direct benefit to Honda, but where Honda were using very valuable resources for work which was overwhelmingly to Rover's benefit. This applied not only to the technical assistance and training programmes, but also to the substantial R&D involvement in projects like SK3 and SK5, both of which were intended to provide products unique to Rover. Honda did of course get paid for the work done and technical assistance given, but that was not what they were in business for.

Under the new regime at Rover we had seen, at last, a real desire to learn from Honda. This was a complete reversal of position; from the early years when there was a rejection of Honda's offered assistance; through the late 1980's when there was a reluctant and grudging acceptance of Honda's insistence that we change our ways; to the current situation where there was a positive desire to learn how to do things better. This combined with the recognition that action was essential if there was to be a future for Rover. It had been a long time coming but, finally, taking advantage of the opportunity to learn from Honda became the natural way and the benefits were starting to come through. The excellent working relationship which had been established between John Towers and Mr Irimajiri was also underpinned by the fact that Iri-san was the Honda Director on the Rover Group Limited Board, while John was the Rover Director on the Honda of the UK (Manufacturing) Board.

Early December found us in Tokyo for the first top level meeting of the new regime. It was a good, constructive meeting and was mainly significant in that it was the first time that Honda ever showed any interest in 4x4 vehicles. It was only very tentative at this stage, but started to develop later. A training programme for Rover people at Honda America was also agreed in principle. This programme involved sending people to the Honda car plant in Ohio for a stay of about a month, during which time they would work as an integral part of the Ohio team. Eventually about 100 people went on this programme and provided a foundation of knowledge and experience which was disseminated through the company.

There had been very serious discussion about this programme before it was formally established. The argument was, however, internal to Honda. No-one was against the idea in principle, the debate was whether it should take place in America or in Japan. The supporters of Japan as the venue argued that this was the only way in which the pure experience of the Honda way could be delivered; going to the USA risked a double dilution of the message. The supporters of the American route accepted that risk but argued that the greater ease of communication between American and Brit would more than offset that possible disadvantage. In the end the American route prevailed and it was certainly a success.

One point which was registered at the meeting was that Rover was having some difficulty with the economics of the SK3 and SK4 projects. There was no discussion of the subject, however the point was registered. It would emerge again at a later date. The SK3 project was really very unusual in that Honda agreed to do all the concept engineering of the car for Rover alone, they were not interested in the product for themselves at this stage. They would of course be paid for the work but, as they certainly did not run Honda R&D as an external design consultancy, it was a good example of the support that they were prepared to give Rover. The idea of the SK3 was to provide Rover with a smallish car based upon a shortened R8 platform. This was seen as a low investment route to providing some solution to the small car problem which had existed and confounded Rover since the early 1980s.

The challenge was how to replace the Metro. There had been a project under development in the mid 1980s, designated AR6, which was an all-new supermini. The economics of this were extremely difficult and the project did not survive the management upheaval of 1986. The difficulty was temporarily avoided by installing the K-Series engine in the Metro which was later rebranded as the Rover 100, but the underlying problem remained. There really was no solution to the small car problem, which had low unit margins requiring very high volumes, which in turn generated the need for high investment. In addition, Rover's desire to move upmarket added to the problem as there were serious concerns about whether a market of sufficient size existed for a high-priced small car. The SK3 concept was intended to solve this problem by moving the product up the size and price scale, and to minimise investment by the carryover of much R8 componentry and production equipment. Even so, this approach did result in a high design cost for the car which was intended to be priced between Metro and R8.

When we got back from Tokyo and prepared for the Christmas holiday the relationship seemed to be in good shape and moving constructively again. Work was going on at high speed on the SK1/SK2 projects and the build at Cowley; the project teams were working well; there were all sorts of problems, but solutions were found and we were all very enthusiastic about the car. We were now developing new agreements for SK1 and SK2 to reflect the completely new circumstances, so there were these new battles to be fought. Even the battles over the Concerto build quality had at least settled down to a running skirmish and we seemed to be providing Honda with an adequate supply of product. It all appeared to be heading the right way.

Chapter 17
1992: SYNCHRO GOES LIVE
Honda Europe begins to play a more significant role

1992 then turned out to be a somewhat unsettled year. It started with the ongoing concerns which Honda had with Rover's profit performance. As a result of their 20% shareholding in Rover Group Ltd, Honda had to account for their share of any losses in their published accounts. Rover Group Ltd, in which Honda had their shareholding, was less profitable than the parent company Rover Group Holdings Ltd in total. The larger organisation encompassed investments in such companies as Leyland-DAF, Unipart and the North American sales company alongside Rover Group Ltd. Honda was itself suffering from depressed profits as a result of the recession in the world motor industry, combined with their heavy exposure to the effect of the strengthening of the Yen against the US$. This made them understandably sensitive to having to exacerbate their financial results with their share of Rover's problems.

There was quite a bit of talking going on, with Finance Director Tony Rose and his team keeping Honda aware of our year end performance. While it did not cause really serious problems between the companies, it remained as a background sensitivity in the relationship. It did highlight one aspect of the Shareholders' Agreement which had always puzzled me, which was the 20% shareholding. In the days before British Aerospace, when Mike Carver and I had been discussing a possible shareholding with Honda, they had always been emphatic that, if they were to participate, the level of holding would have to be less than 20% to avoid them having to consolidate the results. I had therefore been surprised that the issue did not, to my knowledge, arise during the 1989/90 discussions which resulted in the 20% shareholding. It remained an unexplained mystery, and they continued to reflect Rover Group Ltd losses in their accounts.

Early in the New Year the organisation began to get sorted at Rover and Alan Curtis was appointed Managing Director Product Supply, taking over from John Towers who was now Managing Director Rover Group. I had a new boss again. Alan and I had known one another for some years, back to when he had been Personnel Director with Harold Musgrove, and we got on well. Although things were going well on the Synchro project, we were having continuing problems with the economics of the SK3 and SK4 projects. Behind this was Mr Miyake, President of Honda Motor Europe since Mr Iida's departure the previous year. Mr Miyake was a forthright character and was always very concerned about Rover's spending plans and what he saw as attempts to 'run before the ability to walk in a quality manner' had been established.

Some fairly contentious meetings were held at this time with Mr Miyake, to try and negotiate better terms for Rover on the Honda supplied items and services for the SK3 and SK4. This was not successful and led to long lectures from Miyake-san, accusing us of creating the problems ourselves through over-expensive investment plans. This was all happening against a background of reduced market sizes and declining car volumes, leading to poor profit performance. Maintaining the product plan was a problem under these circumstances. Added to all this was a continuing uncertainty about British Aerospace's long-term staying power and its intentions as the owner of a motor manufacturer. This was a constant concern, even though they were really non-intrusive as owners, and the Rover management was allowed great independence within the British Aerospace organisation.

Into all of this broke a great surprise, the sudden announcement that Mr Irimajiri had resigned from active participation in the management of Honda for reasons of ill health. As he was generally seen as the heir apparent, it was unexpected, and the cause of considerable regret to all of us at Rover, who had regarded him as a good friend of the relationship. It has to be recorded, however, that once again we never did manage to find out exactly what was the reason for his departure. It was a somewhat confusing situation for us; on the one hand we were told that the reason for his departure was sudden ill health, which made us fear the worst for him; then, when we tried to find out how serious the problem was, we received messages which were far from clear. To this day the reason for his departure and subsequent reappearance as President of Sega, the computer games company, remains unexplained.

Iri-san was immediately replaced as a director of Rover Group Ltd by Mr Yoshihide Munekuni who, like his predecessor, was an Executive Vice-President of Honda. He was elected to take over the Irimajiri role as the senior man responsible for the relationship and thus John Towers' face-off. Mr Munekuni was not really known to any of us. Unlike Mr Irimajiri he was a commercial man and had spent some time running the US company. We were keen to get him involved in Rover affairs as soon as possible. Because of the unexpected nature of the change, however, he was not able to pay a visit until the summer, some four months after assuming the role. Prior to this visit, Honda announced major organisation changes which confirmed Mr Munekuni's position. Mr Miyake was to be responsible for all automobile activities in Europe, including product. This was in addition to his role as President, Honda Motor Europe. Mr Miyake explained the changes to me and asked if I understood the nature of his new dual role. When I said that it was not absolutely clear to me, he replied that he was pleased to hear that, because it wasn't clear to him either!

Meanwhile we carried on arguing about the Synchro Agreements which now numbered four separate parts; a licence agreement covering the vehicle; an agreement for the engines being supplied from HUM Swindon to Rover; and two body panel agreements, one for panels and sub-assemblies supplied by Rover to HUM and one for smaller sheet metal components supplied from

Japan to Rover for use in both versions of Synchro. The arrangements needed for the type of joint projects represented by Synchro and Theta - which had shared tooling and suppliers for common components, but with the two vehicles being built in different locations - were extremely complex if total chaos was not to ensue. We found plenty to argue about and there were a couple of times when my old friend and sparring partner, Shuko Hayashi and I had major fallings-out. With him now resident in Reading it was much easier for us to keep our arguments on the boil, which we did with enthusiasm.

In July, Mr Munekuni made his first visit. This went well, and was mainly spent familiarising him with the Rover plans, and making sure that the Rover position on key issues between the companies was explained. It was not a meeting for serious negotiations. Because of his background, Mr Munekuni was interested to establish whether there was anything which the two companies could do to collaborate more on the sales front, an area which had, up to now, been outside the collaborative fold. This did eventually lead to something but not at this time.

A little later the decision was made to discontinue the SK3 project as we could not make it financially attractive enough to get it through the British Aerospace Board. Honda R&D had done quite a lot of work on the concept and we paid them for that and called it quits. Although it was the end of the SK3, its successor, designated R3, emerged the following year and was launched in October 1995 as the new Rover 200. The R3 will come back into the story later, but for now the demise of the SK3 did at least give Shuko Hayashi and I one less thing to argue about. We were already beginning to have serious disagreements about the amount and method of payment for the R&D work if the project had come to fruition. Its demise did not, however, solve the product problem which now returned for the time being. Despite all of this, work did continue on the SK4 project (Theta), the styling of which had been firmed up. I was personally not happy with the degree of differentiation between the Honda and Rover versions, which was much less than on the two Synchro versions. Because of the financial problems with the project, there was great pressure to minimise the investment, and limiting the unique visible component content was a way of achieving this. It was the wrong way in my view.

One positive follow-up from the Munekuni visit was that we set up a formal round of meetings called the Planning Group, which was intended to provide a regular basis for discussing matters of mutual interest. As it involved Rover and Honda Europe, everyone was UK based which meant that it could meet about every two months. It was Mr Miyake's idea and became a key element in the management of the relationship. It was the Planning Group which was the forum used to sort out the engine strategy for Theta, which resulted in the car having all Rover engines except for the 1.6-litre automatic transmission unit. This was the derivative which provided the core vehicle with the maximum commonality between the two versions and thus provided the design link engineered by Honda R&D. Honda would, I'm sure, have much preferred to supply all the 1.6-litre engines as they did on R8, but accepted the Rover position with quite good grace. The other aspect of the project was that Rover insisted on having a 4-door version as a replacement for the Rover 400. The 4-door Concerto had not been a success in the market and we stopped production of it for them long before the 5-door.

We thus had the complete reversal of the original R8/YY situation where the 4-door was done by Honda with Rover initially not wanting to know. This time Honda didn't want to know and so Rover was left to develop the 4-door on its own. What had happened, of course, was that the sales performance of the early Rover 400 had been about what we had forecast. It really took off, however, when we fitted the traditional radiator grille as a facelift. Initially this was done to the 4-door only and increased the volume by about 30%. It also caused some irritation at Honda. Because of the joint nature of the programme and us building the Concerto for them we had a provision in the Agreement that we would jointly discuss facelifts for either marque. We had in fact done this but at the time the radiator grille was not planned. Unfortunately, this got lost in the larger discussions around the Memorandum of Understanding and the changed strategy for Synchro and Theta. Honda were not amused when the facelift was launched with only minor changes to the Concerto 4-door and a very new and successful look to the Rover 400. Apologies were made, but it was this sort of happening which the Planning Group would help to avoid. To be absolutely fair, we were all taken by surprise at the outstanding success of the grille idea and very quickly had to follow up by carrying the change over to the 5-door model.

We finally got the Synchro Agreements sorted out to enough mutual satisfaction to get them signed. It was very much 'born in the vestry' as the Accord had already started production at HUM Swindon and the Rover 600 was due to start at Cowley early in 1993. We were still getting to grips with the SK2 project to install the Rover turbocharged petrol and diesel engines into the Rover 600. Honda continued to show no interest in diesel engines, although this was to change in the fairly near future. We were now also getting the early messages from Mr Munekuni indicating interest in the Land Rover Discovery for sale in Japan and the USA.

Chapter 18
1993: BRITISH AEROSPACE HEADS FOR THE EXIT
Honda go 4x4, the emergence of R3 and the appearance of BMW

During the latter part of 1992 and into 1993 we were, at their behest, in very active discussion with Honda on the possibility of them selling the Discovery through their sales networks in Japan and the USA. This really was new. In the past Honda had expressed little interest in the 4x4 vehicles whenever we had, from time to time, raised it with them. Several things had happened to change this situation. The key one was that the market for this type of vehicle had begun to take off in both countries, and Honda were at a major disadvantage in not having one of their own. They had actually been selling some Jeep models in Japan but initially, I believe, more as a gesture to the Americans, probably at the behest of the Ministry of International Trade and Industry, which was the Japanese equivalent of the British Department of Trade and Industry, but far more powerful.

Shortly after we started discussions, Honda informed us that they were doing a similar deal with Isuzu, but for America as well as Japan, and were also to supply Isuzu with cars to sell in Japan. Isuzu had given up car production and were now concentrating on 4-wheel drive and commercial vehicles, where they were much more successful. We were getting ready to launch Discovery in both markets through our own sales companies and networks. It was a bit of a challenge at first, but our sales companies in both markets were small and the potential of access to the Honda sales organisation in both markets had an initial appeal. The suggestion from Honda was that they would sell the vehicles through the Verno network in Japan and the Acura franchise in the US. Both of these were their upmarket networks and so seemed suitable.

We succeeded in coming to agreement in principle regarding Japan quite quickly, agreeing to make some very minor changes to the vehicle and to badge it as the Honda Crossroad. In this way Rover Japan's position selling the Discovery was protected and they were happy with the situation. The USA was much more difficult. The basic problem was that some of our own dealers had committed to invest heavily in setting up specialist Land Rover outlets because they were going to get Discovery, and they would not be amused to find the powerful Acura network selling the same vehicle, even if the name was changed. The other element to the problem was that Mr Amemiya, who was 'Mr America' for Honda, kept emphasising how keen he was to get the vehicle but steadfastly refused to give any volume forecast more than about 1500 a year. As we were then selling more Range Rovers than that through our own small network we could not understand, nor work up any enthusiasm, for the idea. It was particularly inexplicable to us, as the Acura network in the US was the one which Honda had set up in 1985 to sell its upmarket cars such as Legend, and which was then selling over 100,000 cars a year.

This whole discussion went on and on, and round and round. It became a rather Alice in Wonderland situation, with us saying that the only grounds we could have for considering the idea seriously would be if they were talking volume levels which we could not ignore and which we would expect the Acura franchise to produce. Their argument was that if they only sold a limited number, it shouldn't upset our existing network. It was one of the relatively few occasions over the years when I really did have difficulty with Japanese thought processes and logic. In the end we said no, as the whole thing was just too vague to put at risk the plans which had been put in place with Land Rover North America. Honda really were quite upset when we told them no, but it couldn't be helped. It also has to be said that, although the arrangement in Japan was still in place in 1996, it was not very successful and Rover Japan sold far more Discoveries than Honda did Crossroads.

Whilst this was going on, a totally separate set of discussions started, which were of more fundamental importance. Early in the year we commenced highly secret discussions about the possibility of a closer relationship, including the possibility of increasing Honda's shareholding. The basic stimulus for this initiative was the approach of August 1993, which signalled the end of the Government's 'golden share' period, after which British Aerospace was allowed to dispose of Rover Group Holdings, should it so desire. The indications were that it would so desire, as it was difficult to see how a car company would ever be part of the British Aerospace core business. The investigations by Honda were explained to people as the development of benchmarking information. Indeed, much very useful comparative data was generated as an important by-product.

The alternative product front was quite active at this time, stimulated by discussion in the new Planning Group meetings. We had told Honda that we were resurrecting the small car project, but in a very substantially changed form to the earlier SK3 project. The new concept, code named R3, had some links to the R8 Rover 200 but with significant changes to, and redesign of, the suspension. The result of this new concept design was a lower cost vehicle compared with SK3, and one which generated an economically viable programme. It was also encouraging as it was the first substantial new car project to be engineered by Rover for many years.

In the middle of this positive period in the relationship we suddenly had a little confrontation of the type which did boil up from time to time. The public launch of the Rover 600 took place in April, closely followed by the launch of the Swindon-built Accord in the UK (early production Accords had been left-hand drive models for the continental markets). The Rover 600 launch had gone well and then, one Friday evening, I had just arrived home from the office when I received a phone call from our public relations department. They had just been contacted by a journalist who had received the Accord launch press pack from Honda UK (the sales company). It included a very aggressive price comparison between the Accord and the Rover 600: "did we have any comments?" We did indeed, but not for publication! The phone line to Shuko Hayashi at Reading really hummed and harsh words were transmitted. Honda Motor Europe claimed not to have any knowledge of the details of Honda UK's launch publicity.

A damage limitation exercise got under way, with apologies from Reading. It would have been a stupid action at any time, given the joint nature of the Synchro project. It was particularly unfortunate that it should happen when so many important things were beginning to be discussed. I was very cross indeed, as we had earlier established a direct link between the public relations departments to ensure that the timing of launch activities did not clash, enabling each company to receive the maximum possible media attention. The upset died down but there were bitter feelings in many areas of Rover. The incident was seen as a deliberate reaction to the fact that the Rover 200 and 600 had been seen by the media as more attractive cars than their Honda counterparts.

Behind all this, the discussions on future ownership, including Honda Tokyo's review of Rover's operations, together with the benchmarking activities, continued largely undisturbed. The Honda Motor Europe team, with Mr Miyake's new overall responsibilities, was becoming established and developing its own thoughts. The new Planning Group meetings began to get interesting. We soon found ourselves discussing with them, at their instigation, the possibility of us supplying them with diesel engines for installation in the Accord and Honda 'Theta', along with the supply of a Honda badged version of R3. Both of these developments were encouraging as Honda had never before used someone else's engine in one of their cars. So for them to consider such a thing, along with the use of someone else's design of car as their own, represented a major breakthrough. The relationship had come a long way. Honda R&D in Japan remained less than enthusiastic about diesel engines, but the European operation recognised that having diesel-engined cars was a necessity if they were seriously to develop their presence in the European market. By this time even the UK was beginning to have a significant market for diesel cars.

As a lead into the diesel exercise, we agreed in principle to supply them with some diesel-engined Concertos to enable them to get some experience in this market. The agreement had to be provisional because we had to get Peugeot's agreement for the use of their engine in a vehicle which we would supply to Honda. We had used the Peugeot engines in the Rover 200/400 because our own L-Series engine was not ready at that time. As a result, we had developed a very good relationship with them in the mid-1980s. As well as the Rover 200/400 engines, we had done deals with them for the supply of the smaller diesel engine for Metro and the use of their MA gearbox design which we modified and built as the R65 transmission to go with the K-Series engine.

The Peugeot President, Monsieur Calvet, had always been very supportive of the relationship with Rover but was a vociferous opponent of the advance of the Japanese car industry into Europe. A condition of the engine deals had been that we would use them only in Rover vehicles. However, when we asked them about supplying Peugeot-engined Concertos to Honda, somewhat to my surprise they were quite enthusiastic, clearly seeing a possibility for direct supply to Honda at a later date.

Discussions continued on all fronts, but Honda was not really enthusiastic about increasing its shareholding at this stage. In August there was a pleasant interlude when Mr Kawashima - the retired President who was, with Sir Michael Edwardes, the founder of the relationship - paid a visit to Cowley. It was very nice to see him again and for him to see that the relationship was blossoming.

During this period, when we were in ownership discussions with Tokyo, Mr Matsuda, who led for them, had asked us to consider building the Accords for them as well as R3, so that the Swindon capacity could be devoted to Honda 'Theta'. This had not been moved ahead significantly when the message came that the British Aerospace Board wanted to reconsider the situation regarding the position reached with Honda. The shareholding talks would be put on hold temporarily. No sooner had this message been transmitted, which did not seem to present Honda with any problems, than the Sunday Times broke with a story about the proposal to build Accords at Cowley. Each side took the position that the leak must have come from the other. I never did find out and, as so often, by the Tuesday it was dead as a news item with both companies denying it.

BMW made its first approach to British Aerospace in September, a fact of which I was in ignorance, although I did hear rumours. The offer was evidently not attractive enough and was rejected. In early October, we were off to Tokyo for a Simpson/Kawamoto meeting which resulted in the recommencement of the shareholding talks, which then proceeded with a more positive attitude on Honda's part than had previously been apparent.

As a follow up to the 1985 story about my unhappy experience with the *Financial Times* we now had a re-run. The business magazine *Fortune* wanted to do a major article on collaboration between Japanese and European companies, and asked to interview someone who was familiar with the Rover-Honda story. It fell in my lap. In due course a young lady arrived accompanied by a photographer. The interview went well and we then removed ourselves to the car park so that I could be photographed by a Rover 600, then the most recently launched fruit of the relationship. The photographer seemed to take several rolls of film with several cameras and from every angle. I thought that, at the very least, there should certainly be a good photograph as a result. Eventually the article was published. It was excellent, we got good coverage and there weren't any personal comments. There didn't need to be. The photograph chosen, out of what seemed like the hundreds taken, had been taken from ground level, looking upwards with a fisheye lens. The result was that it did nothing for the Rover 600, which is a handsome car. In addition, it did rather exaggerate what was, in reality, only a very slight thickening of my waistline. Once again, the personal comments of colleagues were most unkind. The media had struck again.

The Synchro project resulted in the Rover 600, which was launched in 1993 and manufactured at Cowley. Designed to be an executive car, it was perceived to be too expensive, which damaged its sales prospects.

A Honda Accord (Rover 600 equivalent) with a Great Western Railway locomotive, number 7029, Clun Castle. The tag line is 'born in Swindon', associating Honda's new manufacturing plant with Swindon's long tradition of building steam engines.

The start of manufacture at Swindon marked the end of Honda production at Longbridge. The last Concerto to come off the line was given a big send-off, with both Rover and Honda engineers present.

29 September 1989 (above and below), hatchback and saloon styling models of a new Rover 400 (HHR) which would also be produced as a Honda Civic. Alternatively known as 'Theta', this would be the final project of the collaboration.

Despite the BMW takeover, the HHR project went ahead and the Rover 400 was launched in 1995.

Spot the difference.

Top: Land Rover Discovery.

Launched in 1989, it quickly became popular both in the UK and overseas markets, including the USA.

Bottom: Honda Crossroad.

Honda realised they were unrepresented in the growing 4x4 market. In 1993 Rover Group agreed to let them sell a limited number of Honda badged Discoverys in Japan.

Honda President Nobuhiko Kawamoto with a Honda Civic, built at HUM Swindon, at the Paris Motor Show in 1994.

On his retirement, John was presented with a model Boeing 747 by Japan's national airline, JAL, in honour of his 'frequent flier' status. From now on he would have to travel 'standard' instead of 'executive' class and he expressed his shock to his family at the contrast between the two.

A few years later, in 1998, John Bacchus chats with his old friend and sparring partner, Shuko Hayashi, on the occasion of the latter's retirement.

The high regard in which John was held by his negotiating partners is evident in this retirement gift, a beautiful Cloisonné enamel tray, which is inscribed 'FROM ALL OF YOUR FRIENDS AT HONDA, JANUARY 1995'.

Chapter 19
1994: THE TWILIGHT OF THE GODS

The discussions continued, alternating between London and Tokyo, until we reached a stage in January 1994 whereby Honda had established emphatically that it would not go beyond a 47.5% holding. British Aerospace really wanted to dispose of Rover, and great efforts were made to persuade Honda to go further, but to no avail. They were keen to play a more significant role in the management of Rover but were not prepared to take control and ownership. They were certainly advised that there had to be the risk that British Aerospace might receive a better offer. This advice was given both formally and informally but to no avail. Honda was advised that its position did not meet British Aerospace's aspirations to exit from Rover, or at least to divest themselves of any management responsibility whilst maintaining only a minority shareholding. Nevertheless, in January 1994, Honda firmly stated this as its final position, which was to be formally conveyed to the British Aerospace Board and considered at its next meeting.

It was at this point that BMW made the offer that British Aerospace couldn't refuse. It had been conveyed a few days before the Board Meeting and this time was financially very attractive. The existence of this new offer from BMW was, of course, kept very secret within the British Aerospace management; and so the summons to come into the office at Bickenhill on the evening of Sunday 30 January, there to be given the news of the new ownership, was, to put it mildly, quite a shock for many.

Once the shock had worn off the next question was – what happens now about Honda and all the active and planned joint projects? Honda had been told of the situation by George Simpson, who had gone straight to Tokyo after the British Aerospace Board Meeting to explain the situation to Mr Kawamoto. He evidently received a very frosty reception from Mr Kawamoto who was definitely not happy with the news and stood by the Honda position. Whilst it was understandable that he should be upset, as Honda was building its European strategy on the foundation of the relationship with Rover, the possibility of such a situation arising had been repeatedly stressed to him.

Rover now had real concerns. Every Agreement which we had with Honda provided for either party to have the right to terminate if the other were to be taken over by another motor company. All of a sudden, this provision, which had been seen as a useful 'poison pill' at the time of the Ford affair in 1985/6, became a potential threat.

I thought that BMW were probably aware of the situation as, shortly before the Board meeting, I had been asked to go to London to brief British Aerospace's solicitors in the City on the existing agreements with Honda. I now presume that this was to enable the information to be given to BMW. At the time, the reason given was to ensure that they (the lawyers) understood the situation in the context of the discussions with Honda regarding increasing their shareholding.

There were not only the existing Agreements to think about; in addition we were still in negotiation on the programme for putting the Rover turbocharged petrol and diesel engines in the Rover 600 and for the Theta project, the replacement for the Rover 200/Honda Concerto. Both projects were well advanced but the final details on both remained to be resolved. For a little while there was some uncertainty about what Honda would do and, of course, what the new owners would want to do.

The initial Honda reaction was that there was no possibility of any further collaboration; they saw themselves as being in far too direct competition with BMW, particularly in the USA, to want to collaborate with them. Despite statements to the contrary, this attitude appeared to be reciprocated by BMW. The situation was rather tense for a short while and the media had great fun as they obtained quotes from various Honda people not in a position to speak authoritatively on the subject, threatening all sorts of action against Rover. In fact, after a brief period of uncertainty, Honda went to some lengths to emphasise that their anger was aimed at British Aerospace and, to a lesser extent, at BMW but not their Rover colleagues. This meant that the day-to-day operational activities carried on with a minimum of disturbance.

Nevertheless, the structural and strategic questions still had to be resolved. This involved several trips to Tokyo and New York for very high-level Rover/Honda/BMW discussions which finally came to a conclusion in principle at a meeting at Cowley in April, with the details being resolved in May. The result was that the Cross-shareholding Agreement was to be unwound, and arrangements would be made to continue existing and active projects. These consisted of the installation of Rover engines in the Rover 600 and the Theta project. An agreement was also reached during 1995 for Rover to supply its L-Series diesel engine for Honda to install in the Accords built at Swindon.

From my point of view, all that remained for me to do was to sort out and finalise the Agreements which were necessary to achieve the stated objectives. This was done and I took my last Honda-related trip to Japan, journey number 88, to arrange for their signing. In January 1995, I retired after 25 years with the company.

CONCLUSION
Reflections from the vantage point of 1996

So, as the old, very bad taste joke says: "Never mind that, Mrs Lincoln, how did you enjoy the play?"

The conclusions must be my own and come from one who was always a great believer in the importance and potential of the relationship. The writing of a record such as this brings back memories of past arguments and difficulties, both within British Leyland/Rover and with Honda. It raises the question – was it the right thing, after all? Trying to give an answer is not easy when the subject in question has formed such an important part of one's life, for so many years. Nevertheless, I will try to answer it as honestly as I can.

There can certainly be little argument that British Leyland needed a collaborative relationship with some other motor manufacturer in 1978. The record of product delivery from 1980 onwards enables comparisons to be made quite dispassionately (or at least relatively so). For nearly all of this period, I was closely involved in the new product activity and so was in a position to judge what was happening. On the in-house programmes, despite the strenuous efforts of many dedicated people, we proved unable to deliver the necessary level of quality and reliability unless there was a very substantial, direct Honda involvement in the design, development and production processes.

We really did need them and their assistance and, when we eventually accepted that fact, there was a fundamental change in the culture of the company which fed through into an improvement in the public perception of Rover and its products. We were, however, a long time getting there and wasted a lot of time and goodwill, from our customers and from Honda, whilst we were on the way. At the root of this situation was, I believe, a deep-seated problem which existed from the formation of BLMC back in 1968, and probably even before that. This problem, at the core, was a shortage of highly skilled, highly competent automotive engineers.

This may seem to be a strange thing to say about a company which had a reputation for engineering excellence and included among its alumni such world-famous automotive engineers as Sir Alec Issigonis and Spen King. The company did of course have a number of very high-grade design engineers. We really did have the flair and ability to produce excellent concept design. It used to incense Honda that, when we added our touch to the joint vehicles, the result was that the Rover version was seen to have more style than the Honda version. What it lacked, however, was the depth of excellence in detailed engineering which is such a feature of the German and Japanese industry; the concentration on *doing* everything right, of planning it so it *would* be right, and controlling the delivery process to ensure that it *was* right, was not there.

The result of this was that things didn't work properly, or they broke, or they fell off, or they rattled. In addition, the vehicles were often quite difficult to build which exacerbated the quality problem. Why didn't we solve these problems ourselves? Why go running to the Japanese? We had been building cars since 1896, Honda hadn't started building four-wheeled vehicles until the early 1960s and launched its first real car, the Civic, in 1972. The answers to these questions, which basically face a large portion of our manufacturing industry, are still being sought. Many improvements have been brought about in recent years and the performance is greatly improved but the real impetus had to come from outside.

How about Honda as a partner? Could we have done a better deal or series of deals with someone else? The 'what if' questions are impossible to answer. The relationship lasted for 16 years and remained in place for some time after the purchase of Rover by BMW. More significantly, until that event, it continued to grow and evolve its form and structure in an organic fashion, so the conclusion must be that it was achieving something. The fundamental problem with the relationship was, of course, money. I recently came across a quotation which sums up the situation splendidly. It is by George Bernard Shaw, from his play *Man and Superman*: "You can be as romantic as you like about love Hector, but you mustn't be romantic about money."

There were such vast amounts of money changing hands, particularly from Rover to Honda, mainly for component supplies, that it was bound to be a source of trouble. It was, constantly. The claim within British Leyland/Rover was always that the components supplied by Honda were excessively expensive and that they designed components which were high cost, even if they were not the supplier. There was some truth in this, but not to the extent claimed by many people in the company, particularly in the earlier period. A key problem was that Honda insisted on being paid for supplies from Japan in Yen. As the years went by the Yen/£ exchange rate became increasingly unfavourable to the UK. This had to create problems, and it did. A key feature was, however, that the quality was absolutely first class and that was something we desperately needed. Honda certainly made money from the things which they supplied to Rover, the question is whether Rover got value for its money. Honda did not design low-cost cars, they did however design cars which were of the highest quality and reliability and that was Rover's greatest weakness during the 1980s.

There were, of course, downsides. Rover did come to rely for too long on Honda for technical input, and for many years used Honda R&D as a support when it should have been developing its own resources. It should be recorded that, in the early days of his Presidency, Mr Kawamoto frequently expressed his wish to see Rover developing its own R&D activities with more urgency. This did not happen until the 1990s, when it led to cars like the MGF and a new Rover 200.

Nor were Honda perfect technically. Their suspension systems were capable of improvement, certainly for European tastes and conditions. Rover frequently improved on the tuning of the Honda suspension designs to its own benefit. Honda engines, although jewels in many ways, always developed their torque too high up the rev range; this was always a bone of contention between the companies and can be seen by comparing the performance characteristics of the Rover K-Series 1.6-litre engine with the Honda dual overhead cam unit which it supplanted in the Rover 400. The K-Series has slightly lower peak power but develops more torque at lower revs. This does make for a more flexible drive, with less gear changing.

They could also be very difficult to deal with on matters technical as well as commercial. There was one way to do things and that was the Honda way. This was frequently disputed but rarely conceded. Honda R&D were not very open to alternative ideas when they had made up their minds about something. There were also times when they did use their position of strength in the relationship to their commercial benefit, but not as often as people liked to make out. They were very clever, tough negotiators and we certainly learned a lot from them, I know that I did.

In the end, I do believe that both companies benefitted substantially from the relationship. Honda made money and got an easier way into European markets at a time when it was concentrating its efforts on the development of its position in North America. For Rover Group, the benefits were more fundamental. It survived as a car maker, became respectable again and established a foundation on which to build a future.

Triumph Acclaim (Bounty)

Rover 200 (Acclaim Facelift or SD3)

Rover 800 (XX)

Rover 200 (R8)

Rover 600 (Synchro)

Rover 400 (HHR or Theta)

Honda Ballade

Honda Ballade

Honda Legend

Honda Concerto

Honda Accord

Honda Civic

Appendix 1
FOCUS ON THE CARS
Ian Elliott

Ian Elliott is well placed to tell the other side of the story – how the cars were launched and marketed. He worked for British Leyland (under its numerous name changes) in marketing and public relations between 1973 and 1991. This is an abridged version of a supplement to the John Bacchus narrative, written in 1996. The Bibliography includes books of interest for those who would like to delve further into the detailed history of the products which came out of the British Leyland/Rover Group/Honda collaboration.

1981: TRIUMPH ACCLAIM, CODENAME 'BOUNTY' [Honda Ballade]

Launched on 7 October 1981, the Triumph Acclaim was advertised with the strapline: *Totally equipped to Triumph*. This reflected the high specification, with features such as a 5-speed gearbox, a tachometer, twin remote control door mirrors, a digital clock and even a headlamp levelling control using a hydraulic system. Unusual in this sector at the time was the availability of a semi-automatic transmission. This used a torque-converter and a 3-speed gear train with conventional helical gears, with changes effected by multi-plate clutches. Originally called Hondamatic, it was appropriately labelled Trio-matic for the Acclaim. Even more unusual in the lower-medium sector (and still not universal by 1996) was the availability of factory-fitted air-conditioning.

In round numbers, £70 million was invested into Cowley during the preparations for Acclaim production, although other models were to benefit from many of the new facilities. There was a new paint plant which utilised technologies such as cathodic electro-prime and clear-over-base metallic finishes. Four high-output automated press lines were installed to cope with the Acclaim's monoside pressings and the two-at-a-time method of pressing panels such as doors. They were the biggest in Western Europe at the time, with a 15 foot bed width and sliding bolsters allowing die changes in minutes rather than hours. Bodyshell assembly, although not as highly automated as the lines set up at Longbridge for the high-volume Metro, nevertheless used state-of-the-art robot welding for the underframe. An automatic framing jig carried out the critical geometry-fixing operation of welding the sides and roof panel to the floorpan. Honda supplied body pressing dies and welding equipment to the value of about £4.5 million.

For final assembly, a track in the former Cowley North Works was refurbished, introducing a new technique for installing the engine which would become known as 'stuff-up' because it involved lifting the power units and suspension assemblies up into the suspended bodyshells, instead of the body being lowered onto the mechanicals. This method gave better control of the process and provided easier access for bolting up the various

APPENDIX 1

mountings and would become the norm in subsequent years. There was also a computerised end-of-line roller test facility which allowed dynamic setting of steering lock settings and wheel alignment. This was an important feature on the Acclaim because, like several other Honda-based designs, it had adjustable alignment at both ends. The roller tests also encompassed power, braking and emission checks. A Vehicle Electrical Test System provided the last stage of computerised inspection of the finished vehicle.

Although the speed of the Acclaim programme limited the amount of local content which could be used, efforts were made to use local suppliers where possible. All the obvious bolt-on items, from wheels and tyres to batteries and exhausts came from UK or EEC suppliers. The radiator, which had to be adapted to meet Honda specifications, was sourced from British Leyland's in-house radiator plant. One of the factors which improved the Acclaim's passenger leg room compared with its sister, the Honda Ballade, was the canny adaptation of an off-the-shelf front seat frame that was normally to be found in the contemporary Ford Cortina. Following a value-added assessment of the total EEC content of the original Acclaim, it was calculated to be 70% of the vehicle's price.

Initially launched with three derivatives - HL, HLS and CD - the Acclaim range was expanded into the lower price range by the addition of an L version in the autumn of 1982. In its first full year of UK sales (1982) the Acclaim sold 42,188 units, enough to achieve 2.71% of the total market and claim seventh place in the top sellers chart, just behind the Vauxhall Astra. Even with a substantial degree of in-house competition from the Maestro (launched in March), the Acclaim's 1983 sales remained strong, with 38,406 units and a 2.2 % market share, sufficient to hold eighth position in the charts. Total UK Sales from launch to the final registration in August 1985 amounted to 99,753 units. Over 30,000 Acclaims were exported to European markets during its brief production life, with France taking the largest share at some 10,000 cars.

The publicity strategy deliberately minimised references to the Honda connection in advertising and consumer literature. Understandably, the motoring press had other ideas and tended to major on the novelty of Britain's national carmaker building a Japanese car under licence while giving rather less space than usual to details of the product itself. Nevertheless, the general tenor of launch coverage was positive. There had already been much debate and discussion about the British Leyland/Honda link and it was accepted by most people as a *fait accompli* by the time the car was launched.

The Honda equivalent, the Ballade, had been revealed in Japan in August 1980, so there was little point in trying to keep the appearance of the Acclaim secret. The people responsible for preparing the Acclaim launch material had the unusual luxury of having complete, fully functional cars available four months before launch that could even be driven around without camouflage.

By the time October arrived, the only people still making a significant fuss (and then only off the record) were those UK component suppliers who didn't initially have any involvement in Acclaim.

Press Comment - Triumph Acclaim:

Autocar magazine took an Acclaim HL on a 1000-mile tour of the country at the end of August 1981, over a month before the launch, to canvass public opinion about the car and its origins. Amongst the 200 people interviewed, there was broad agreement that the Acclaim looked Japanese, but only 22% said that the Japanese content would put them off buying the car. Asked if it could be considered British, 55% said no. Nevertheless, 73% of the respondents thought that the collaboration was a good idea.

Motor magazine did a 12,000 mile test with an Acclaim HLS and published its report in early December 1982, combining its experience with feedback from 40 Acclaim-owning readers. Phillip Turner's conclusion was:

> 'When it was first announced that BL were to build a Honda model in Britain, there were many doubters around who wondered out loud whether the British version of a Japanese car would be as well built as the Japanese version. Judging by this Acclaim, the answer is indeed yes, it is just as well put together and as reliable as its Japanese sisters ... As for me, I liked the car. It was comfortable, quiet and fun to drive.'

The Daily Telegraph was a key opinion former for a substantial section of the Acclaim's target market. Its motoring correspondent John Langley noted:

> 'In feel and appearance, it is typical of the better sort of Japanese car, though BL Cars has been trying to convince itself that it is also a "traditional Triumph" whatever that was. Within the tight limits imposed on them, the BL engineers have indeed managed to incorporate some development tweaks to increase the Acclaim's acceptability to European motorists. As a result, the Acclaim is noticeably livelier than the then-new Ballade I drove in Tokyo a year ago. It also has better seats and, on smooth surfaces, a better ride. It is well made and well equipped and I fancy that plenty of British motorists will find its blend of lively performance and good petrol economy appealing.'

1984: ROVER 200, CODENAME 'SD3' [Honda Ballade]

The first Rover 200 Series was announced on 19 June 1984. It was a landmark car, defining the structure and image of British Leyland/Rover Group's model range for the next 16 years. Its codename was 'SD3', but, as referred to in the John Bacchus narrative, it was known internally as the 'Acclaim Facelift'. Although the Triumph Acclaim had successfully allayed the company's concerns about public reaction to its Japanese connections, applying this principle to the Rover marque sparked a new debate on the subject. The advertising strapline for the launch was: *Born to be driven, Bred*

APPENDIX 1

to be Rover - which hinted that it might be necessary to establish the car's credentials in this area.

The first derivatives launched (known as 213) were fitted with a Honda 1.3-litre engine in S, SE and Vanden Plas versions. The Rover 213 had several technical novelties. The 1.3-litre engine featured three valves per cylinder (two inlet, one exhaust) operated from a single overhead camshaft by two sets of rockers. This configuration was not new for Honda. Kiyoshi Kawashima (who became President of the company in 1973) had designed the 3-valve, 146 cc four stroke E-type motorcycle engine which first set Honda on the road to success back in 1951. It was not the norm in the UK, however.

The 216 made its debut on 12 March 1985, powered by a 1.6-litre S-series engine designed by Austin Rover. For the 216S and SE models, there was a carburetted 85 bhp unit similar to that in the 1.6 Maestro and Montego derivatives, while the 216 Vanden Plas EFi and the 216 Vitesse had the benefit of multi-point fuel injection and 103 bhp. Since there was insufficient width to install the 1.6-litre engines with the Volkswagen transmission used for Maestro and Montego, the stronger but more compact Honda-designed PG1 transmission from the 2-litre Montego was used. The 216 Vanden Plas replaced the 213 Vanden Plas, as a result of which the latter became one of the rarest of models, with an official run of only nine months.

The suspension design, carried over from the Honda Civic, was idiosyncratic. At the front, the engine bay width was maximised by using slimline, damper-only struts, with longitudinal torsion bar springs in place of the usual coils. Rather than a conventional long torsion bar, however, Honda created a co-axial bar and tube arrangement of virtually half the normal length. When it came to the rear suspension, it used a coil-sprung, dead beam axle located by trailing arms and a panhard rod. The right hand trailing arm was rigidly fixed to the axle beam, the other had a free swivel bearing. The objective was to allow a very elegant anti-roll bar installation inside the axle beam while avoiding unwanted roll stiffening effects. Unfortunately, the speed of the SD3 programme meant that the Austin Rover engineers didn't have any opportunity to tune the suspension as they had with the Acclaim. At the launch, the 213 was criticised for its ride quality, and in particular for a corkscrewing effect arising from the rear suspension. By the time the 216 was launched nine months later, a pragmatic solution had been found and implemented on all 200 Series models.

At the British Motor Show in October 1986, a facelift (or rather, a bootlift) for the 200 Series was revealed. The most significant change was a new bootlid which opened down to the bumper level between the rear lamps. The interior was also upgraded with new seating, door casings and centre console, all in a similar style to that of its new 800 Series sister model.

At the time, the key medium sector volume models – Maestro and Montego – were being built at Cowley. The Rover 200 therefore played an important role in balancing the production capacity at Longbridge, which would otherwise have been totally dependent on the smaller Metro and Mini models. The first of several re-arrangements of the Metro body plant was undertaken to accommodate Rover 200 bodyshell production, which used a mix of robotic and manual weld processes. This was the company's first bodyshell facility to have a single weld monitoring system covering the entire line. Final assembly took place in the Longbridge Car Assembly Building known as CAB2 which had been built in the 1960s to expand production capacity. Among the vehicles manufactured here had been 1100s and Allegros. From 1982-84 it was used to assemble the last 45,000 examples of the Morris Ital which had been displaced from Cowley by the Maestro and Montego ranges.

With cleaner, more 'international' styling and a broader engine choice than the Acclaim, the new small Rover enjoyed a steady growth in UK sales volume during its five-year run. In its first full year (1985) it sold 43,668 units, representing 2.38% of total market share. By 1988 this had climbed to 58,890 (2.66%), and in 1989 it combined with the new R8 model introduced in October to total 68,316 (2.97%).

Press Comment - Rover 200 (SD3):

Motor magazine was cautious in its first description of the new 213 models. It was very critical of the original suspension, but praised its distinctive styling:

> 'The Rover's ride is disappointing, and falls short of the high standards set by the Maestro and Montego, whose absorbency it does not share ... The Rover 200 is better equipped to succeed for Austin Rover than the Acclaim was, but this is just as well as the notchback competition consisted of just the Volkswagen Jetta when the Acclaim was launched. The gaggle of similar models now includes the Renault 9, Volvo 360 saloon, Lancia Prisma, Ford Orion and Alfa 33 ... The Acclaim's replacement has one major advantage over the opposition. Unlike the Orion, it is not merely a mutation of another model in its manufacturer's range - an XYZ model with a boot - and this should give it the individuality it needs to succeed.'

Motor did a new write up following the 216 launch, when they carried a detailed explanation of Rover's revisions to the suspension :

> 'The improvement at speed over the same route was marked. The vertical jerking is no longer a concern and the car is much more composed on poor surfaces. Its relatively short wheel travel compared with, say, a Montego, stops it being a class leader for ride quality but happily it now does the job competently.'

1986: ROVER 800, CODENAME 'XX' [Honda Legend]

Unusually, the Rover 800 was the subject of a fairly detailed press briefing at the end of October 1985, eight months ahead of the official launch. This was carried out to coincide with Honda's reveal of the Honda Legend just before

APPENDIX 1

its debut at the Tokyo Motor Show. For the event, journalists were ushered into the recently completed Canley Design Studio run by stylist Roy Axe. The official names had not been decided at this stage and the only photographs available were of the new M16 2-litre engine. No-one was allowed to photograph the cars, instead several accurate artists impressions were published. These were based on the journalists' brief recollections of what they were shown.

The public launch took place on 10 July 1986, with an advertising theme of *Engineering in a Finer Form*, which had some resonance with the traditional Rover image of excellence in engineering but side-stepped the issue of its Anglo-Japanese parentage. At the bottom of the range were the 820E and SE which were powered by the single-point injection 120PS, though no price or performance data was issued since they had yet to complete the homologation process. In the middle were the 820i and Si (both with a 140PS multi-point injection engine). There was much for engineers to appreciate, such as the 4-valve per cylinder provision across the range, all-round disc brakes and two different state-of-the-art power steering systems. The 4-cylinder cars featured a new 'positive centre feel' power rack developed by Austin Rover and supplier TRW, which had a solid connection between column and pinion at the straight ahead position. There was also a V6-powered 825i fitted with Honda's speed sensitive steering, which picked up road speed via a gearbox drive to reduce assistance at higher speeds.

The launch stock, however, largely comprised top of the range Rover Sterlings. Rover claimed that the flagship Sterling model was the best-specified car available in Britain. With a wealth of luxury features such as a fully powered adjustment for all the driver's seat settings, along with a memory facility for up to four users to dial in their personal seat and door mirror settings, it certainly scored high marks for showroom novelty. Special warnings were issued to dealers to keep an eye on battery charge; by the time a salesman had enthusiastically demonstrated the power seats on a showroom car to a dozen customers, there was likely to be a shortage of amps. Even the split rear seats had power fore-aft and recline adjustment; but this really only served to move from adequate to inadequate legroom and the feature was quietly dropped within a couple of years.

Many industry-leading manufacturing technologies were adopted for the XX manufacturing programme. It marked a considerable advance in the use of Computer Integrated Engineering (CIE) whereby a central design database was used to drive all the project activities. With over 330 workstations networked across the company, Rover claimed to have the largest computer aided design installation in the European car industry. The Low Pressure Sand (LPS) casting technique used at Longbridge to produce M16 cylinder heads took place in the first high volume foundry of its type in the world.

Cowley, where assembly took place, also enjoyed a substantial infusion of the latest technologies. Consisting of more than 400 different panels, the Rover 800 body range was the most complex ever produced here, while the monoside panels were the largest single panels ever handled in all the years of production in the Body Plant. There was a new, automated bodyshell inspection cell, using 62 laser cameras to carry out 96 direct and computed checks for dimensional accuracy. Another small but important innovation was pre-heating the bodyshell before injecting hot wax into the various cavities. This allowed the wax to penetrate deeper before 'freezing' thus improving the corrosion protection.

The Rover 800 also saw the introduction of an important new technique in final assembly known as 'DODO' (doors off, doors on). Once the bodyshell had been painted, the doors were removed to progress down their own assembly line, providing the workforce assembling the car with easier access around and inside the body. This enabled the operators to work at a comfortable height, protected the doors from the risk of damage on a busy assembly line and enabled the electro-mechanical assemblies to be quality-tested before the door was re-united with the car near the end of the track. Like the 'stuff-up' technique mentioned earlier, this manufacturing procedure would become the norm.

Press Comment - Rover 800:

The relationship between Austin Rover and the media at the time of the XX launch was not at its most harmonious.

Car magazine, however, was the only publication to go for he jugular, stating in its editorial that it had been too lenient on previous new cars from the company and putting forward the familiar theory that it was necessary to be cruel to be kind. They were certainly cruel. After criticising the pre-production press cars for poor assembly quality (delays on component supplies had forced extensive use of mock-up parts) and attacking all the power units for having peak torque too high in the rev range, they said:

> 'But, even ignoring quality control, the Rover 800 is a disappointment. It does have its worthwhile features – notably nimbleness and an attractive cabin – but it's not the winner Austin Rover wants. Or needs.'

Motor, the more influential weekly magazine, was fortunately more positive. Comparing the Rover Sterling with a BMW 525i, a Mercedes 260E, a Lancia Thema V6 and Ford Granada Scorpio, it said :

> 'On looks alone, the Brit is best. The really low scuttle, inches lower than the Ford, gives it a distinctive, sporting look, complemented by the sharpest and most elegant profile in the business ... the Sterling takes the attack on rear-drivers one step further, by being the fastest-cornering of the pack ... The interior was designed to set the car apart from its rivals and it does.'

It was March 1987 before *Motor* published a brief road test of the 820E, then priced at under £11,000. They summed up:

APPENDIX 1

> '... the lowest-priced big Rover has much going for it. Throw in the fact that it is an easy, undemanding car to drive smoothly, it rides and handles smoothly and looks smart, and it's hard to escape the conclusion that this is one of the best buys at the lower end of the executive sector.'

In the USA unfortunately, where the car was marketed as the Sterling, the reaction was not enthusiastic. In September 1987, the *American Consumers Union* reported that the car it bought for testing developed 15 faults:

> 'From the very outset, our Sterling betrayed a lack of quality control that would be a disgrace in a car costing one quarter as much. As the mileage built up, more and more problems arose. It was hardly the "car without compromise" that the sumptuous sales brochure promised. The Sterling 825SL was intended to be a blend of Western and Eastern philosophies, an amalgam of high-tech Japanese precision and traditional British elegance. Unfortunately, the Sterling inherited more than buried walnut and Connelly leather from its British side. It also seems to have inherited the sloppy fit and finish for which the British car industry was once so notorious.'

Over the next decade, many developments would continue to be made to the Rover 800, both technical and cosmetic, continuing right up to 1996. Most notable, perhaps, was a major facelift (codenamed R17) which took place for the 1992 model year. As well as technical improvements, this heralded the re-introduction of the grille into Rover styling. Market research in America and Europe had consistently suggested that customers would like a stronger, more characteristic front end style. So, as part of the facelift styling, a modern interpretation of the traditional Rover grille (last seen on the big Rover 3.5 litre P5B of 1967-73) was developed. Although the R17 programme brought in many all-round improvements, there is little doubt that it was the powerful symbolism of the grille that really hit the jackpot, particularly in the UK. The grille would subsequently be adopted on all Rover models across the range.

The *Daily Mail* said of the grille:

> 'Rover has reached back into its proud history to give the new 800 series executive saloon a touch of British tradition. The grille is derived from those which graced Rover saloons and coupes from the Fifties to the Seventies. In those days Rover boasted that each of its models was "one of Britain's fine cars". It counted the Queen and Queen Mother among its most valued customers.'

1989: ROVER 200/400, CODENAME 'R8' [Honda Concerto]

All new models are important in their own right, but the Rover 200 (codenamed R8) carried with it so many change factors that it must be regarded as a very significant product milestone in Rover Group history. It was introduced at the October 1989 London Motorfair (held bi-annually at Earls Court). As

APPENDIX 1

well as the new model range, the press and the public were introduced to the new company identity. The company had recently passed out of government ownership into the hands of British Aerospace and change was afoot. Although the parent company, British Leyland, had changed its name to Rover Group in 1986, it was not until 1989 that the name of the trading group which interfaced with the public changed from Austin Rover to just Rover.

This new generation of Rover 200s consisted of 5-door hatchbacks, which were powered by the first completely new range of in-house engines to emerge from the company in decades in the form of the K-Series engine. The 214 range was fitted with the K-series 1.4-litre twin cam unit (with 16-valve single-point injection developing up to 95PS). The 216 range carried Honda's 1.6-litre single cam unit (16-valve developing up to 116PS). This was just the start of the R8 family. It was part of the new Honda-driven quality strategy to bring in derivatives progressively. From a manufacturing point of view, the Rover 400, launched on 28 March 1990, was simply a 4-door booted version of the 200, but every effort was made in marketing activities to promote it as a distinct car positioned well above the 5-door car.

At the 1990 Motor Show at the National Exhibition Centre (NEC) in Birmingham, 3-door versions of the 200 series were launched with unique monosides that owed nothing to Honda. An unusual side window treatment, rather reminiscent of the Ford Sierra XR4, gave them a distinctly sporting air. They started with a new entry-level 214S, powered by the single cam 1.4-litre 86PS K-Series engine which had made its debut in the Rover Metro. A similar 5-door model was available. The 214Si 3-door had the normal twin cam 95PS engine. Then there were two 216 GTi 3-door models; an entry level model fitted with the 116 PS single cam Honda unit, and a more sporty version badged 'Twin cam' to emphasise the 130PS power unit. 1991 saw this 'hot' GTi being used for the new Dunlop Rover GTi one-make race series.

The next major step in the growth of the R8 family came in March 1991 when diesel versions were launched, followed at the end of November by new 420 models.

Rover went on to produce three models which had no Honda equivalents. At the March 1992 Geneva Show, the 'Tracer' was unveiled, badged as the 200 Cabriolet. This 4-seat soft top was the first production convertible Rover since 1947. It came in 214 and 216 versions, with the option of power operation for the 3-layer hood. This was followed at the October 1992 Paris Show by 'Tomcat', otherwise known as the 200 Coupe. An ingenious combination of a twin glass panel targa-top coupe roof with a cabriolet bottom half, it was launched with 1.6-litre, 2-litre and 2-litre turbo engines. A Turbo Coupe was designated as the twelve millionth car to be built at Longbridge since production began in 1905. It proved itself to be the fastest Rover to date when a team of enthusiastic Rover volunteers used it to set 37 land speed records at the Millbrook test track, averaging 138.43 mph over 24 hours, and recording a maximum speed of 156 mph. The trio of sporting models was completed by the 'Tex' introduced at the 1994 Geneva Show as the Rover 400 Tourer. This was not a tourer as in soft-top, but instead more in the BMW 'touring' sense of an estate car with the emphasis on life-style rather than carrying capacity.

To achieve all of this required a huge amount of investment. Over £350 million was spent at Longbridge, with a further £50 million at the Swindon Pressings plant. Unfamiliar management techniques were introduced such as 'project teamwork'. Multi-disciplinary teams took the car from design through development and into production in one methodical process, with manufacturing staff and suppliers being involved from the outset. In manufacture, too, a new system of production teams was introduced, with responsibility for quality, productivity and materials being devolved to shop floor level.

The marketing strategy was designed to tap into popular culture. The launch TV commercial for the new Rover 200 series was based on the wedding scene from the Dustin Hoffman film *The Graduate*. In Rover's version, the hero dashes to the church in a 200 rather than an Alfa Romeo, just in time to save his girl from a loveless marriage. Providing the soundtrack was the theme song *Up Where You Belong* from the film *An Officer and a Gentleman*. A different treatment was needed for the 400 launch, since it was to be presented as a distinct product in its own right. The topical theme of *glasnost* was chosen in an era when the cold war was thawing, leading to improved relationships between the West and the USSR. It featured a young British diplomat driving to Moscow in his new Rover 400. To film the closing frames, a car was actually driven into Red Square by special arrangement. The strapline was *Class without the Struggle*; to illustrate this advertising posters showed the car against a backdrop of Russian monuments to the class conflict.

UK sales of the Rover 200 Series climbed steadily from its launch. In 1990 (its first full year) 53,200 were sold rising to a peak of 80,300 by 1994. Export sales followed a similar pattern, rising from 24,400 in 1990 to 56,200 in 1994. France took the major share of exports closely followed by Italy and Spain. The more exclusive Rover 400 began its UK career with 20,500 sales in the nine months of 1990 and peaked a year earlier than the 200 by selling 33,200 units in 1993. Exports, mainly to France, Italy and Portugal, similarly rose from 11,200 in 1991 to a maximum of 18,100 in 1993. The grand totals for all R8 models between 1989 and 1995 were: UK sales 579,200; Export Sales 328,300 (all figures rounded to nearest 100 and not including post-1995 sales).

Press Comment - Rover 200/400 (R8):

Every effort was made to give the R8 the best possible press launch and it certainly paid off. It may not have had quite the messianic zeal and trumpet-

APPENDIX 1

blowing that had accompanied the patriotic launch of the Metro in 1980, but the coverage of the new Rover 200 was consistently warm and positive in a way that hadn't really been experienced since the 1963 launch of the P6 Rover 2000.

Car magazine, never one to favour Rover without good reason, said :
> 'Rover has achieved all it set out to do with the 200. It has distanced it from the competition, yet kept it accessible. You get a car high on refinement, quality and driver appeal. It's not perfect, but it is desirable. At last, Rover has got it right.'

What Car? magazine ran a comparison test between a Rover 200 and its main hatchback rivals. Not only the journalists, but also the consumer panel, unanimously picked the 200 as their favourite, something that had never happened to any of the company's previous products. The summary read:
> 'At long last, Rover has a winner, a real winner. Looking through the test there is much talk of electric windows, sunroofs, electric mirrors, central locking – the Rover has none of these but it doesn't matter one bit, for this car oozes quality … it's as if you were comparing a BMW with an Escort - you have to keep rechecking the price list to make sure it is actually so cheap.'

Autocar and Motor tested the 214GSi, and noted :
> 'Rover's new middleweight is not just good enough to beat the Escort -class front runners, it outshines the top-spec versions in several key areas, notably ride/handling, build quality and performance.' When they tried the Honda Concerto, they added: 'After driving the Rover, you feel the Concerto has something missing - it's as much character as anything. Driving the two cars together indicates the Rover as the original, the Honda as the re-badged clone.'

The all-important national newspaper pundits were equally impressed by the R8. *The Observer* correspondent wrote:
> 'Driving several versions, I warmed quickly to the car for its relaxed responsiveness. It has a directness of feel which makes it pleasurable as a 'driver's car' without ruffling passengers' comfort.'

The Times correspondent observed :
> 'It is perfectly timed to enter a lower medium sector full of tired-looking products…'

Finally, closer to home, the *Coventry Evening Telegraph* summed up:
> 'The new Rover 200 hatchbacks bring job security to Rover factories, a powerful new weapon in the fierce showroom sales wars and a delightful car for motorists who want comfort and practicality to go hand in hand with luxury, style and low running costs … never has a new Rover product made such an impact on me or many of my colleagues.'

APPENDIX 1

Speaking of the 400 model, the *AA* reported in a 1991 car test:

> 'When Britain's last major car maker decided to badge everything as "Rover", it was seeking to reassert that image of quality and reliable, sound engineering that was the original connotation of the Viking emblem. People who had bought the SD1 or even an early 800 might have thought otherwise. However, it certainly seems as if this latest marketing ploy is more than mere hype. The latest 200/400 range is well-designed - it doesn't expect early owners to complete the development programme as previous BL offerings did.'

1993: ROVER 600, CODENAME 'SYNCHRO' [Honda Accord]

Announced on 7 April 1993, the Rover 600 Series underwent a deliberate, phased introduction of models and options. Honda's batch production logistics and walk-before-you-run quality rules were followed. The first models were the 620Si, SLi and GSi which all used the mid-range 2-litre 131 PS engine. A few months later the 620i was released, powered by a lower-tuned 115PS version of the same 16-valve engine. Towards the end of the year, the 623iS and 623GSi models were brought on stream, fitted with the much more powerful 2.3-litre twin cam. These were all Honda aluminium engines, featuring twin balancer shafts and a hydraulic rear engine mount for extra smoothness and quietness. Models fitted with Honda's electronically controlled 4-speed automatic gearbox also had electronically controlled valving within the hydraulic mount to damp out any idling speed tremors from the torque converter.

There was a variety of new safety features. Side impact bars in the doors were standard across the whole range. Some of the higher specs also featured anti-lock braking and air bags. The early 620i models were fitted with neutral grey plastic bumpers, as an obvious visual and cost differential from the painted bumpers of all other models. Dealer and customer reaction to this was so negative that most cars had their bumpers painted by the supplying dealer and production models quickly went to painted bumpers in January 1994.

In May 1994, a revised model range was announced in response to market changes largely driven by a new income tax regime for company cars. A driver's airbag became standard on all models, with a front passenger airbag optional higher up the range. Another new option was cruise control and the security system was upgraded.

At the Amsterdam Motor Show on 31 January 1995, the diesel versions of the 600 were revealed. This was also the debut of Rover's own new direct-injection turbo-diesel L-Series engine. Incorporating the latest Bosch electronic drive-by-wire fuelling control, the power unit developed a vigorous 105PS, backed up by 210 Nm of torque at only 2000 rpm. This delivered class-leading performance and economy so it was not too surprising that Honda was to reverse its usual role and become a customer of Rover, installing the L-Series in its Accord range.

Some £200 million was invested in the Cowley plant to establish a new integrated facility to make both the 600 and 800 ranges. The former Morris Motors site, now known as Cowley North and South Works was closed and the complete process, from body-in-white to final assembly, was concentrated in the former Pressed Steel factory. Instead of being spread across 222 acres, production now took place on 112 acres, reducing the need for lengthy and inefficient conveyor systems, truck deliveries and buffer stores. The Rover Swindon Pressings plant was also upgraded in 1992, receiving an investment of £56 million to install and commission two new 5000-ton transfer presses. These would produce panels for both the 600 Series and the Honda Accord, now being produced at Honda's own Swindon car plant. Extensive sub-assembly of 600 Series body sections also took place at Rover Swindon. An inventory management method known Just-in-time (JIT) was introduced. The idea was that goods should be received from suppliers 'just in time', thus reducing the need for expensive storage. There were also new roll-on, roll-off pallet systems to eliminate much of the old, inefficient fork-lift truck handling of supplies.

The marketing campaign was designed to position the Rover 600 as a premium product. Unfortunately, the initial price comparison with the Honda Accord helped to over-emphasise this in price terms. It also has to be accepted that, despite fine engineering and build quality, both the 600 and the Accord found themselves up against the best-ever mainstream competitive products in this sector, backed by far bigger marketing budgets. A time of lingering recession was not ideal for trying to establish what was effectively a new premium brand at the top of the upper-medium sector. Perhaps tempting fate, the launch TV commercial for the Rover 600 played on its exclusivity by showing a 600 driving in splendid isolation in various exotic settings. The finale suggested that you were as likely to see another 600 as to see lightning strike in the same place twice.

UK sales in its first three years ran at 14,500, 23,400 and 23,600, which unfortunately made this prophecy all too true. Unusually, but in line with declared Rover Group objectives, the 600 achieved export volumes that were higher than its UK sales during its second and third years, with 24,400 and 36,800 respectively. The leading market in both years was Italy which responded to the car's elegant styling. Other major markets were France, Spain and Japan.

Press Comment - Rover 600:

One thing that the press pundits all agreed about was that Rover's Design Studio had pulled off their finest achievement to date in giving the 600 a distinctive Rover identity.

APPENDIX 1

Autocar and Motor commented:
> 'And what a fabulous job Rover has done ... The Rover is all elegance and grace yet at the same time handsome and distinctly arresting ... the 600's styling is a success - it's classy, handsome.'

Car magazine was also unusually enthusiastic:
> 'No question. It's a winner. We're talking class - and that's what the upper echelons of the M2 sector are all about - the 620SLi exudes it. Above all, it imbues the driver with a sense of it's-good-to-be-here well-being that its rivals can't match. It has style, it has image, it has class.'

Typical customers for the 600 were more likely to read the quality papers then the car press, but they would have found similarly upbeat comments here.

The Sunday Times:
> 'The 600 is fast, good-looking and quiet and fits comfortably into Rover's tradition of quality and good taste.'

The Observer
> 'Sampling several versions on the route from Buckinghamshire into the Cotswolds, I relished their verve and fluidity. The cars have light, precise steering, tidy cornering manners and a smooth gearchange, plus a comfortable interior and ride.'

1995: ROVER 400, CODENAME 'HHR' [Honda Civic]

This would be the last of the joint Rover/Honda cars due to the takeover of Rover Group by BMW during 1994. It was codenamed 'HHR' and is also referred to as 'Theta' in the John Bacchus narrative.

The launch of the Rover 400 in March 1995 was a very different scenario from that of the R8 which it replaced. The arrival of BMW of course was significant, but there were a number of other factors. Honda was building the sister car, the Civic (codenamed 'HHH'), at its own plant in Swindon; and, for the first time, Rover was to use its own engines in virtually all of its derivatives. The 416 models introduced the new 1.6-litre version of the K-Series engine to the marketplace. This, and the longer stroke 1.8-litre units used in the MGF sports car, had been evolved from the 1.4-litre twin cam design by using ingenious part-wet, part dry-sleeved cylinder liners that allowed a bore increase from 75mm to 80mm. Although producing slightly less peak power than the 1.6-litre power unit fitted to the Honda Civic, its maximum torque was higher and occurred at a much more usable 3000 rpm compared with the Honda's 5100 rpm.

The only exception was the 416 SLi Automatic, which retained updated versions of the Honda automatic transmission that had been used in the previous R8 216 and 416 models. It was a Honda requirement that at least one derivative in the Rover range had to be mechanically common to the Honda equivalent (in this case the Civic) to form an engineering datum point.

APPENDIX 1

The 416 SLi automatic was deliberately chosen as a low-volume derivative that would cause minimum disruption to Rover's sourcing and manufacturing strategies. Initially, at least, it was very much the odd one out, as even details like the seat frames were different to those of the rest of the range.

From a marketing point of view, the launch of the Rover 400 was very difficult. The hard truth was that there would be a long overlap with the outgoing R8 versions, alongside the fact that there were going to be unavoidable gaps in supply. For example, the booted 4-door Rover 400 had to be the first R8 type to be phased out, but the last to be replaced because Rover's unique 4-door version of the HHR type couldn't be brought on stream until 1996. A tricky course had to be steered between giving customers guidance and not revealing commercially sensitive product information. In the end, it was decided to declare the complete HHR range at launch, even though they would not all be available immediately for purchase.

Sales also got off to a slow start, and the word coming back from the network was that many potential customers were holding back because a new version of the Rover 200 (codenamed R3) was expected shortly. This car was to be quite different from the existing R8 Rover 200, being smaller and more compact, and it was not planned for launch until early 1996. A snap decision was taken to bring forward the reveal of R3 to the London Motor Show in October 1995. This surprise tactic worked very well, gaining positive coverage, as well as successfully unblocking demand for the 400 from people who now understood that the two cars were in different market segments.

Press Comment - Rover 400 (HHR):

In general, the 400 was well-received but didn't arouse the pundits in the way that the R8 version had done. It performed well in road tests, with journalists agreeing that it was ahead of the Civic and most other rivals when it came to comfort. The biggest problem lay in Rover's attempt to position it against larger cars such as the Ford Mondeo, Vauxhall Cavalier/Vectra. The car didn't quite have the interior package size or the external presence, even in extended 4-door form, to carry this off.

What Car? magazine said :

> 'Ride quality is also first class. Different ratings to the Civic's suspension have produced a ride that copes with potholes and poor road surfaces in equal good measure.'

Car magazine was again in a curmudgeonly mood, and while admitting that there was nothing wrong with the car, made a big cover splash of it as their 'Lemon of the Year', purely because, in their opinion, it was too closely based on the Honda Civic.

A young John Bacchus (centre) arrives at the airport after the press and dealer launch of the Austin Allegro in Spain in 1973. Due to an air traffic control strike, British Leyland had to hire a chartered flight to get participants there in time. They thus unexpectedly enjoyed the novelty of a trip on a new Boeing 'jumbo' jet.

At the 1975 Motor Show in Earls Court, the Leyland Cars Division lays out the multiplicity of the company's brands on a series of stands which stretch into the distance - Austin, Morris, MG, Jaguar, Daimler, Rover, Triumph ...

In 1988, the Rover 800 was launched in the USA as the Sterling with its own logo. Above, the stand is prepared for the big day. Below, men in busbys and soldier uniforms portray a not very subtle message about Britishness. Unfortunately it was British unreliability that did for the Sterling, which was withdrawn from the American market after only a few years.

Appendix 2
JOHN BACCHUS
Career Timeline

Rolls-Royce Aero Division

1959-60 *Commercial Sales Division*: Finance Assistant, Pricing

Ford Motor Company

1960-61 *Corporate Finance Staff*: Senior Analyst, Product Pricing
1961-63 Supervisor, Product Pricing
1963-64 Supervisor, Product Programme Analysis
1964-66 *Product Planning Staff*: Manager, Light Truck Range, including Transit van
1966-67 Manager, Truck Component Planning

Chrysler-Rootes

1967-68 *Staff*: Pricing Manager

British Leyland/Rover Group

1968-69 *BLMC*: Controller, Product Development Group
1969-70 Group Manager, Financial Analysis
1970-73 Product Planning Director
1973-75 Director Corporate Product Plans
1975-78 *British Leyland International*: Business Planning Director
1978-79 *British Leyland*: Business Development Director
1979 Project Director
1980 *Jaguar Rover Triumph*: Director Finance and Planning
1980-83 *Austin Morris/Austin Rover*: Director Business Strategy
1984-89 *Austin Rover Group*: Director Product and Business Strategy
1989-91 *Rover Group*: Director Collaborative Strategy
1992-95 Director Honda Collaboration

Retirement

1995-2010 Warwick Manufacturing Group, TVS Group India:
Consultant, Lecturer & Student Mentor
1995-2000 **British Motor Industry Heritage Trust**: Archive Volunteer
2000-2007 Trustee

Appendix 3
A SHORT HISTORY OF COLLABORATION
John Bacchus

One of the things which has emerged while writing this book, is the realisation that collaboration was nothing new to Rover Group and its predecessors.

The Austin Motor Company had a history of product collaboration going back a long way. In the Heritage Motor Centre (*note: the name was changed to the British Motor Museum in 2015*) at Gaydon near Warwick, a very early example can be seen. It is an Austin 'Seven' dated 1910. This is not related to the much-loved ancestor of the Mini, the Austin Seven of the 1920s-30s. The car is a single cylinder Swift which was manufactured in Coventry, but also at Longbridge in an Austin version to fill a product gap - it has a familiar ring.

The interwar years saw the more famous Austin Seven, introduced by the Austin Motor Company in 1922, being built in several countries under different names. The most significant of these arrangements was in Germany where the 'Dixi' was produced. This was an Austin Seven built under licence which became the first BMW motorcar. Shortly after the announcement of the takeover of Rover Group by BMW in 1994, a joint gathering of the senior executives of both companies was held at Museum in Gaydon. The purpose was to enable people to get to know one another and for Bernd Pischetsrieder, Chairman of BMW, to explain how things would be handled. In a charming gesture, he brought the Dixi from the BMW Museum in Munich and presented it to the British Motor Industry Heritage Trust, its spiritual home.

Another notable Austin Seven was the Datsun Seven mentioned earlier in this work. Like the Dixi, this was based on the Austin Seven design but in this case without a licence. Sir Herbert Austin purchased one so that his lawyers could check whether or not it infringed any of the company's patents. It would appear that it didn't since no action was taken and Sir Herbert kept the car. It is now part of the Collections of the National Motor Museum at Beaulieu in Hampshire. The postwar period saw the continuation of the tradition of Austins going to Japan as CKD kits, where they were to be built by Nissan (parent company of Datsun) who were restarting car manufacture now the war was over.

Meanwhile Austin's arch-enemy at Cowley, Morris Motors, was doing a deal with Hindustan Motors in India which led to the Morris Oxford of the early 1950s being built there as the famous (or infamous) Hindustan Ambassador. The Ambassador is, remarkably, still in production in India at the time of writing, although it is many, many years since modern day Rover Group (or its predecessors) gained any benefit from sales of the vehicle. (*note: the Hindustan Ambassador finally went out of production in India in 2014*)

Following the merger of Austin and Morris in 1952 to create the British Motor Corporation (BMC), the theme of collaboration theme continued in new

APPENDIX 3

ways. Arrangements with Donald Healey resulted in the Austin Healey sports cars; co-operation with John Cooper created the sporty Mini Coopers. BMC even designed and built unique cars for other people to sell, as in the case of the little Metropolitan which was initially created for Nash to sell as the Nash Metropolitan in the USA. It was also sold in limited numbers through the BMC network in the UK as the Metropolitan. History must record that it didn't do much for either company, although over 100,000 units were built.

In the 1960s, BMC and Rolls Royce undertook an extensive technical collaboration, which included proposals for Rolls Royce and Bentley models using bodyshells derived from existing BMC vehicles. Rolls Royce wisely decided not to pursue this idea for expanding into lower-priced market sectors. BMC, less wisely, decided to use the work already done to produce the 1964 Princess 4-litre R (with a Rolls Royce engine) and the 1967 Austin 3-litre.

During the 1960s, Rover pulled off a quasi-collaborative coup by purchasing the rights to build the ex-General Motors 3.5-litre aluminium V8 engine. General Motors participated to the extent of allowing Joe Turley, one of its engine experts who was about to retire, to move to Britain and help Rover anglicise the design and production of this superb unit, which was still being successfully manufactured in the UK in 1999.

Standard-Triumph provides another example, building Ferguson Tractors for some years after the falling out between Ford and Harry Ferguson. Subsequently Triumph designed, built and sold the first versions of their Slant-Four engine to Saab for the Saab 99. The engine was used by Saab for some time before Triumph used it in their own Dolomite and TR7 models.

I am sure that more extensive research would reveal more examples. This, however, provides enough evidence to demonstrate that the Honda relationship was in the established traditions of the company.

BIBLIOGRAPHY

This bibliography points readers to publications which contain background to the events described in this book. It also contains books which cover the period following the BMW takeover, which is not part of this story but was, in itself, indelibly influenced by the events which went before.

Axe, Roy; *A Life in Style* (AR Publishing, 2010)
Bardsley, Gillian & Corke, Colin; *Making Cars at Longbridge* (History Press, 2016, 2nd edition)
Bardsley, Gillian & Laing, Stephen; *Making Cars at Cowley* (History Press, 2013, 2nd edition)
Bardsley, Gillian; *Issigonis: The Official Biography* (Icon Books, 2005)
Batchelor, John & Cheetham, Craig; *The Real R3 Story - told by those who were there* (Rover 200 and 400 Owners Club, 2020)
Brady, Chris & Lorenz, Andrew; *End of the Road, BMW and Rover, a brand too far* (Pearson Education, 2001)
Carver, Mike, Seale, Nick & Youngson, Anne; *British Leyland Motor Corporation 1968-2005* (History Press, 2015)
Carver, Mike, Seale, Nick & Youngson, Anne; *When Rover Met Honda* (CSY Publishing, 2008)
Casucci, Piero; *Rover 800 Series* (Automobilia, 1986)
Church, Roy; *The Rise and Decline of the British Motor Industry* (CUP, 1995)
Cowin, Chris; *BMC and British Leyland Cars in Europe and the World 1945-85* (Amazon, 2014)
Cowin, Chris; *British Leyland: Chronicle of a Car Crash 1968-78* (Amazon, 2014)
Cowin, Chris; *British Leyland: Betting on a Miracle 1978-1986* (Amazon, 2019)
Daniels, Jeff; *British Leyland, The Truth about the Cars* (Osprey, 1980)
Dymock, Eric; *Honda, The UK Story* (Dove Publishing, 1995)
Edwardes, Michael; *Back from the Brink* (Collins, 1983)
Gould, Mike; *The Rover Group, Company and Cars, 1986-2000* (Crowood Press, 2015)
Hazelwood, Mitchell; *The Poor Boy Who Created Honda* (1 Down Publication, 2023)
Hothi, Nicola R; *Globalisation and Manufacturing Decline. Aspects of British Industry* (Arena Books, 2005)
Moore, Charles; *Margaret Thatcher, The Authorised Biography. Vol 1 Not for turning* (Penguin, 2014)
Moore, Charles; *Margaret Thatcher, The Authorised Biography. Vol 2 Everything she wants* (Penguin, 2016)
Motor Manufacturing EDC; *Japan: Its Motor Industry and Market* (HMSO, 1971)
Pilkington, Alan; *Transforming Rover. Renewal against the odds 1981-1994* (Bristol Academic Press, 1996)
Taylor, James; *Rover 800 Series, the complete story* (Crowood Press, 2016)
Taylor, James; *British Leyland, The Cars 1968-86* (Crowood Press, 2018)
Taylor, James; *Rover R8, the complete story* (Amberley Publications, 2021)
Thatcher, Margaret; *The Downing Street Years* (Harper Press, 2012)
Turner, Graham; *The Leyland Papers* (Eyre & Spottiswoode, 1971)

BIBLIOGRAPHY (continued)

Webster, Mark; *Assembly. A History of New Zealand Car Production 1921-1998* (New Holland Publishers, 2021)
Whisler, Timothy R; *The British Motor Industry, 1945-94. A case study in industrial decline* (OUP, 1999)
Williams, Karel, Williams, John & Haslam, Colin; *The Breakdown of Austin Rover* (Berg, 1987)
Wilson, Harold; *Final Term, The Labour Government 1974-1976* (Weidenfeld & Nicholson, 1979)
Wood, Jonathan; *Wheels of Misfortune. The rise and fall of the British motor industry* (Sidgwick and Jackson, 1988)
Ziegler, Philip; *Wilson,The Authorised Life* (Weidenfeld & Nicholson, 1993)

INDEX

PEOPLE
Andrews, David 13, 15-17, 19, 21, 24, 26, 51, 80
Anne, Princess Royal 54-5
Bertodo, Roland 66, 95-6
Carver, Mike 21-3, 28-9, 31, 33-4, 46, 68, 80, 82-3, 88, 95-6, 117
Coultas, Fred 7, 106
Day, Graham 76, 80-3, 86, 95-6, 103, 105, 107, 110, 112, 114
Edwardes, Michael 17-18, 21-3, 26, 30-1, 33, 38, 43, 51, 80, 124
Elliott, Frances 88, 96
Fernyhough, Mike 34-5
Hayashi, Shuko 27, 54, 88, 96, 105, 119, 123, 130
Horrocks, Ray 19, 42, 45, 50-1, 53, 77, 80
Iida, Osamu 88, 94, 96, 105, 108, 114, 117
Ikemi, Kiyoshi 14, 19, 20-1, 27, 45, 67, 88, 110
Irimajiri, Shoichiro 107, 111-12, 115, 118
Ishikawa, Fujio 14, 27-8, 31, 82, 87-8, 94
Kawamoto, Nobuhiko 63, 69, 76, 105-7, 110, 112-14, 124, 129, 131, 134
Kawashima, Kiyoshi 18-20, 23, 26, 38, 42-3, 45, 53, 57, 124, 140
Kume, Tadashi 47-8, 55, 57, 63, 68, 76, 78, 86, 95-6, 103, 105, 107, 110
Mackay, John 23-5, 33
Miyake, Shojiro 114, 117-19, 123
Munekuni, Yoshihide 118-20
Musgrove, Harold 26, 39, 55, 65, 67-8, 71, 75, 80-2, 117
Okamura, Noboru 19, 29, 31, 42
Pendry, Mike 69, 79
Rose, Tony 76, 83, 96, 103-4, 117
Ryder, Sir Don 11, 13-14
Simpson, George 76, 95-6, 105, 107, 111, 113-14, 124, 131
Snowdon, Mark 22, 26, 42, 45-6, 50, 63, 70, 77, 80, 82-3
Suzuki, Masami 19, 31, 96
Talbot, Cedric 50, 54
Thatcher, Margaret 11, 26, 31, 75, 81, 95
Thompson, Pratt 23, 27-8
Towers, John 76, 105-7, 112-15, 117-18
Warner, Sir Fred 18-19, 22-3, 46
Wharton, Les 76, 83, 88
Wilson, Harold 11, 26

PRODUCTS
Austin Allegro 13, 22, 141, 152
Austin Maxi 13, 22, 91
Honda Accord 14-15, 21-2, 48, 54, 86, 90, 103
Honda Accord (Synchro) 100, 114, 120, 122-4, 127, 132, 136, 148-9
Honda Ballade (Acclaim) 16, 51, 136-8
Honda Ballade (Acclaim Facelift) 59-60, 63, 65, 69, 79, 83-4, 93-4, 106, 136, 139-41
Honda Civic 13-15, 21-2, 36, 48, 63, 104, 134, 140
Honda Civic (HHH or Theta) 101, 123-4, 128-9, 136, 150-1
Honda Concerto (R8/YY) 84, 94, 97, 99, 103, 106-7, 111-3, 116, 120, 123-4, 127, 132, 136, 144, 147
Honda Crossroad 121-2, 129
Honda Legend (XX) 58-9, 69, 71, 80, 83-4, 87-9, 93, 104, 121, 136, 141
Honda Quintet 49, 52, 54-55, 70
K-Series Engine 64, 66, 68, 70, 84, 89, 91-2, 106, 109, 116, 123, 135, 145, 150
Land Rover Discovery 106, 120-1, 129
Leyland Princess 22, 48-9
Maestro (LM10) 22, 44, 49, 51, 64-5, 69, 85, 91, 138, 140-1
Metro (LC8) 22, 32, 35, 64, 68, 85, 89, 103, 116, 123, 137, 141, 145, 147
Mini 11, 13, 141, 155
Montego (LM11) 14, 22, 37, 44, 49, 51, 65, 85, 90-1, 140-1
Morris Marina 13, 22
Rover 200 (Acclaim Facelift/SD3) 47, 51-3, 59-63, 65, 69, 79, 136, 139-41
Rover 200 & 400 (R8/YY) 66-70, 78-9, 81-91, 93-9, 103-7, 111-6, 120, 122, 132, 136, 141, 144-8, 150-1
Rover 200 (R3) 119, 121-4, 151
Rover 400 (HHR or Theta) 113-4, 120, 128, 135-6, 150-1
Rover 600 (Synchro) 96-7, 100, 105-9, 111-4, 117-26, 132, 136, 148-150
Rover 800 (R17) 102, 144
Rover 800 (XX) 42-4, 47-58, 63, 66-75, 78-90, 93, 102-4, 109, 111, 114, 136, 140-4
Rover SD1 28, 37, 44, 48, 57, 148
Sterling (NAS XX) 57, 69, 87-9, 144, 153
Triumph Acclaim (Bounty) 27-9, 33-5, 38-41, 43-4, 46, 51, 61, 136, 137-9
Triumph Dolomite 22-3, 156

FACTORIES
Canley 27-28, 30-31, 82, 97, 113, 142
Cowley 26, 30-2, 34, 39, 44, 46, 51, 70, 72-3, 77, 82-4, 88-9, 113, 116, 120, 124, 126, 132, 137, 140-2, 149, 155
Longbridge 37-38, 51, 60-3, 69, 82, 84, 89, 94, 98-9, 101, 104, 111-12, 127, 137, 141-2, 145-6, 155
Seneffe 20-1, 28
Speke 27-8, 30-1
Suzuka (Honda) 28-9, 32, 96
Swindon (HUM) 63, 65, 68, 70, 81-2, 84-5, 99-101, 103-8, 113, 118-20, 122, 124, 127, 129, 132, 149-50
Wako (Honda R&D) 22, 48-9, 59-60, 79

159

THE VIKING AND THE SAMURAI

John Bacchus